Walter Sunderland Lewis

The Life of Lives

The Story of Jesus of Nazareth in its Earliest Form

Walter Sunderland Lewis

The Life of Lives
The Story of Jesus of Nazareth in its Earliest Form

ISBN/EAN: 9783337253646

Printed in Europe, USA, Canada, Australia, Japan

Cover: Foto ©Lupo / pixelio.de

More available books at **www.hansebooks.com**

THE

LIFE OF LIVES

OR

THE STORY OF JESUS OF NAZARETH

IN ITS EARLIEST FORM

Oxford
PRINTED BY HORACE HART, PRINTER TO THE UNIVERSITY

THE
LIFE OF LIVES

OR

THE STORY OF JESUS OF NAZARETH
IN ITS EARLIEST FORM

BY THE

REV. W. S. LEWIS, M.A.

AUTHOR OF 'THE GREAT PROBLEM, OR CHRISTIANITY AS IT IS,' ETC.

'This is Jesus, the King of the Jews.'—MATT. xxvii. 37.

THE RELIGIOUS TRACT SOCIETY
56 PATERNOSTER ROW, AND 65 ST. PAUL'S CHURCHYARD
1885

CONTENTS.

PART I.

THE FIELD OF INQUIRY.

			PAGE
CHAPTER I.	Its Special Interest		9
,, II.	Its General Plan		12

PART II.

THE APPEARANCE OF CHRIST.

CHAPTER I.	His Human Lineage	19
,, II.	His Superhuman Origin	23
,, III.	His Proper Rank	26

PART III.

THE MINISTRY OF CHRIST.

CHAPTER I.	Its Solemn Opening	33
,, II.	Its Supreme Importance	38
,, III.	Its Marked Unobtrusiveness	42
,, IV.	Its Unexampled Authority	46
,, V.	Its Unrivalled Power	54
,, VI.	Its Few Helps	63
,, VII.	Its Many Opponents	69
,, VIII.	Its Singular Wisdom	77
,, IX.	Its Highest Point	83

PART IV.

THE PASSION OF CHRIST.

		PAGE
CHAPTER I.	A Change of Voice	95
,, II.	A Change of Attitude	104
,, III.	A Wide Conspiracy	110
,, IV.	A Final Warning	114
,, V.	A Final Prediction	121
,, VI.	The Eve of Betrayal	128
,, VII.	The Night of Betrayal	133
,, VIII.	Unsullied Innocence	141
,, IX.	Inscrutable Depths	149
,, X.	Total Eclipse	157

PART V.

THE RE-APPEARANCE OF CHRIST.

CHAPTER I.	A Double Dawn	163
,, II.	An Impossible Story	168
,, III.	An Eternal Work	173

PART VI.

THE SUMMING UP 181

PART I.

THE FIELD OF INQUIRY.

CHAPTER I.

ITS SPECIAL INTEREST.

WHAT does the Gospel of St. Matthew, taken by itself and considered as a whole, teach us about Christ? In other words, what sort of ideal of Jesus of Nazareth does it present to our thoughts?

This inquiry is interesting on many accounts.

It is so, first, on account of the surpassing interest of the subject discussed. All things considered, no other name can be put in comparison with that of the historical Christ. On this ground alone this Book of St. Matthew's is deserving of special attention. If a writer is worth hearing on any subject, he is worth hearing on this.

The inquiry is interesting, in the next place, on account of the position of the writer. Both as a matter of reputation, and as a matter of fact, that position—whoever he was—is unique. As a matter of reputation, his treatise is almost universally regarded as the very earliest of its sort. As a matter of fact, no similar production has yet succeeded in establishing so early a date. This doubles the interest of his treatise. The first known *Life of Christ* possesses the first claim on our thoughts.

The peculiar complexion of these nineteenth-century times lends further interest to this inquiry. Amongst the many conclusions of former ages which the courage of this age has assailed, have been all past ideals of Christ. Teacher after teacher has risen up of late to set the world right on this point. In no case, however, has the success of these authorities been equal to their ambition. Their very multiplicity, on the contrary, is a sufficient confession that they do not satisfy one another. It is also, of course, a strong additional inducement for reverting to the primary view. Once more let us examine that ancient original, on which it seems so difficult to improve.

Something may also be urged in favour of doing so, on the score of comparative novelty and freshness. This Gospel of St. Matthew has been examined repeatedly in detail; and almost word by word, as it were. Wonderful is the amount of microscopical attention which has been bestowed on it thus. Repeatedly, also, has this Gospel been considered in combination with the subsequent three. Wonderful, again, has been the amount of ingenuity expended in endeavouring to turn these four histories into one. But the same can hardly be affirmed of that method of treatment which we now have in our eye. The writers who have set themselves to treat this pioneer Story of Christ rather by itself than as one of a series, and rather as a whole than as a collection of fragments, are not a numerous class. So examined, therefore, it may not unreasonably be expected to present us, even now, with fresh phases and truths. As a matter of fact, indeed, no serious student of Holy Scripture supposes that either of those other two methods of examining the contents of this Gospel have yet exhausted their stores. Much less, therefore, this more neglected, yet certainly not more difficult, mode.

As a final reflection, it may be worth considering that this is the more orderly plan. Whatever may have come to pass since, this book of St. Matthew's was not presented to mankind, in the first instance, as one of a set. However great, also, its practical value may be when handled as though little more than a collection of fragments, it certainly was not so put forward by the writer himself. Rather, at first, it comes before us distinctly as a separate whole—quite as much so, in fact, as, in a different region, does the very orb of this earth. It is thus, therefore—so it seems to follow—that we ought to deal with it first. Before we do anything else with it, we ought to examine it as such a separate orb.

It is thus, accordingly, that we propose to deal with it in the present inquiry.

CHAPTER II.

ITS GENERAL PLAN.

THE most satisfactory survey of a country is that, as a rule, which is most successful in allowing it to exhibit itself. In no other way can we feel so assured that it will appear to us as it is.

In dealing, therefore, with that important document at present before us, we shall seek from the outset to keep in view a similar rule. We shall endeavour throughout to enable this Gospel to speak for itself.

If this endeavour should lead to a brevity of treatment not always observable in some recent biographies of the Prophet of Nazareth, we do not know that such a result is to be altogether deplored. In any case, it cannot rightly be helped. St. Matthew himself is uniformly pertinent and concise. To be discursive and diffuse, therefore, in dealing with him, would be to misrepresent him throughout.

A more intricate point is the general view which ought to be entertained of his book. In regard to this point it seems especially important to be guided by the writer himself. However artless in certain respects his composition may appear, he must have followed some kind of order in giving expression to his thoughts. If we know nothing of this, how can we judge correctly either of his aim or success? And how can we know this better than by this natural method of, as it were, consulting himself?

Our main inquiry, therefore, in this second preliminary chapter, has reference to this point. Does the Evangelist himself provide us with any intimations respecting his own order of thought?

The 21st verse of his 16th chapter appears to be of much significance in this way.

Its exact language is this:—'From that time forth began Jesus to shew unto His disciples how that He must go unto Jerusalem, and suffer many things of the elders and chief priests and scribes, and be killed, and be raised again the third day.'

In these words, the Evangelist evidently invites our special attention to a certain remarkable change of character in the teaching of Christ at a certain point in His course.

Up to that point he describes Him, by implication, as rarely, if ever, making open reference to the coming catastrophe of His death.

From that point he describes Him as constantly doing so in the plainest possible way. '*From that time forth began* Jesus to *shew* unto His disciples' these things.

Clearly, therefore, we have a distinction here of a very palpable kind, like that between sea and dry land. The topic which is conspicuous for its absence in the one case is conspicuous for its presence in the other.

Clearly, also, we have a distinction here of a peculiarly vital description, like that between darkness and light. *The* topic, on the absence or presence of which everything turns, is nothing less than the violent death of the Man whose life-story is being told.

Altogether, therefore, in this passage we have just that kind of guidance which our purpose requires. It is the Evangelist himself who teaches us thus broadly to separate all that portion of his Gospel which goes before, from all that portion which follows after, this transition-point in his story.

Another passage in this Gospel is worthy of notice in the same connection.

We refer to that in which Jesus of Nazareth is represented as saying of Himself (ch. xx. 28), 'The Son of Man is come not to be ministered unto, but to minister, and to give His life a ransom for many.'

In the first half of this verse, we find Christ describing His mission on earth with reference to His labours or 'ministrations' alone.

In the second clause we find Him speaking of it with exclusive reference to His passion and death.

In other words, according to this Evangelist, on one important occasion at least, Christ Himself openly and expressly divided His whole work upon earth in entire accordance with that primary division of it to which we have already been led.

This is very strong additional testimony to the fundamental character of that division. It is a division which marks, according to Christ Himself, the turning-point of His mission.

This last passage also enables us conveniently to characterize the distinction in question.

Up to ch. xvi. 21, that is to say, we may consider St. Matthew as principally engaged in giving us a history of the MINISTRY of Jesus.

After that verse we may regard him as engaged principally in telling us of Christ's PASSION and DEATH.

Moreover, the division thus summarised at once leads to two others of scarcely less subordinate rank.

On the one hand, e.g., a glance at the opening chapters of the history shews us that they relate to matters of a preliminary description, and that they have chiefly to do, in fact, with the first tidings of Christ's appearance on earth.

We may regard these chapters, therefore, as a kind of prelude to the rest of the book.

On the other hand, a similar glance at the closing verses of this history will shew us that they relate to matters of a supplementary kind; and that they have chiefly to do, in fact, with the marvellous story of Christ's return to this earth.

These verses, therefore, we may look upon as a kind of sequel to all.

We are thus led to the following general view of the order of thought in this book.

Practically speaking, four unequal main divisions make up its whole bulk.

The first of these portions (Matt. i–iv) gives us a brief narrative of the APPEARANCE of CHRIST.

The leading topic of the second portion (ch. v–xvi. 21) is the MINISTRY of CHRIST.

The dominant thought of the third portion (ch. xvi. 21–xxvii. 57) is the PASSION of CHRIST.

The great subject of the last portion (ch. xxvii. 57, xxviii) is the RE-APPEARANCE of CHRIST.

This is how St. Matthew himself practically divides his own book.

This, therefore, is how we shall divide it in our present survey.

NOTE.—In working out these main divisions, the exact order of their constituent chapters and verses has been adhered to throughout; partly in loyalty to St. Matthew himself, and partly in order to facilitate reference to his Gospel without distracting the reader by perpetual quotations of chapter and verse. The particular portion of St. Matthew, however, under consideration in each successive section of this work is always noted at its head.

PART II.

THE APPEARANCE OF CHRIST.

CHAPTER I.

HIS HUMAN LINEAGE.

Matt. i. 1-17.

This biographical sketch, like many others, begins with the lineage of its subject. Who was this 'Jesus Christ' to whom it refers? From what line did He spring?

The answer is given as follows:—He was 'Jesus Christ, the son of David, the son of Abraham.'

To appreciate this answer, we must bear in mind who David and Abraham were, viz., two men pre-eminently distinguished in the sacred Books of the Jews.

They were distinguished, e.g., as being the special objects of God's approbation and favour. Even at the time of the Evangelist's writing, Abraham was remembered as 'the friend of God' (James ii. 23), and David as 'the man after God's own heart' (Acts xiii. 22).

They were also distinguished as men with whose families or direct descendants God had been pleased to connect certain promises of blessing to all the families of the earth. Thus to Abraham He had said (Gen. xxii. 18), 'In thy seed shall all the nations of the earth be blessed.' While of King David, Abraham's descendant, He had further declared, that this promised 'seed' should not only spring from his line, but also sit on his throne.

To assert, therefore, that this 'Jesus Christ' was directly descended from these, was to assert, in fact, that He sprang from the line from which the Christ was to arise.

In support of this weighty assertion, therefore, the pedigree of Jesus is next given at length (Matt. i. 2–17); but, obviously, not in such a form in some respects as modern readers would naturally have expected.

It is equally obvious, at the same time, that the writer himself puts it forward without misgiving or doubt. He may be considered, in fact, to be defying any one who understands the case to convict him of being either incorrect or irrelevant. 'These national documents, understood in our national manner, prove that the pedigree of this Jesus was the appointed pedigree of Messiah.'

Probably this is why the only four women named in this genealogy, viz., Thamar, Rahab, Ruth, and Bathsheba, are all women who happen to be the subjects of special episodes, either for good or for evil, in the national annals. In dealing with acknowledged national data in the national manner, it would be equally natural to mention these, and to mention no other beside.

The form of this genealogy will be found to bear significantly, in the next place, on the question of time.

Special attention is asked to the fact that the 'generations' it contains admit of being broken up into three separate groups of 'fourteen' each (ver. 17).

Attention is also asked to the fact that all three of these groups are made to begin, and therefore the two earlier of them made to conclude, at certain highly critical historical times.

The first group, for example, begins with the person of Abraham; and so, at the time of the first great national promise of the Messiah, and, as it were, of the very foundation of the chosen people and race.

In a similar way the first group ends, and the second begins, in the person of David; and so, at the time of the second national promise of the Messiah, and, as it were, of the very foundation of the chosen dynasty and kingdom.

In a similar way, again; the second series concludes and the third begins, at the time of that great Babylonian captivity, which seemed to be an utter end both of kingdom and race; and the return from which, therefore, was nothing less than a moral resurrection of both.

How fitting, therefore—how fully according to precedent, and how happy a consummation of all—that the termination of the third series of 'fourteen generations' should be marked by so critical an event as the actual appearance of this long-prophesied King!

As well, therefore, in regard to the precise date of His appearing, as in regard to the particular family from which He sprang, this genealogy of Jesus serves to point Him out as being indeed Jesus the 'Christ.'

The expected Messiah could not have arisen from a different line.

The expected Messiah could hardly have been manifested at a more suitable time.

CHAPTER II.

HIS SUPERHUMAN ORIGIN.

Matt. i. 18–25.

AFTER noting the 'time' of the appearance of Christ, the Evangelist proceeds to ask attention to its manner (ch. i. 18–25). 'The birth of Jesus Christ was on' such 'wise,' according to him, as to be well worthy of note.

It was so on account of the unexampled Agency to which it was due.

Mention has already been made, in ver. 16, of the mother of Jesus. We also read there of 'Joseph, the husband of Mary, of whom was born Jesus, who is called Christ.'

It now appears that after the time of her espousal to Joseph, and before their coming together, her husband hears that about her which makes him think it his duty, notwithstanding the explanation which she appears to have offered (see end of ver. 18), to 'put her away.' Whilst debating this point with himself, and planning how to do so in the most considerate manner, if he did it at all, he receives a message from heaven. Some one whom he recognizes as 'the angel of the Lord' appears to him in a dream. This messenger begins by bearing express testimony to his character and descent, and by giving him also an express command not to take the step of which he had thought: 'Joseph, thou son of David, fear not to take unto thee Mary thy wife.' He then vouchsafes him a sufficient reason for this unexpected command—a reason which stated in so many words what we suppose the mother of Jesus to have already stated herself, viz., that 'that which is conceived in her is of the Holy Ghost.' After which he furnishes Joseph with much instruction respecting the child about to be born. Respecting its sex: 'she shall bring forth a *Son.*' Respecting its name: 'thou shalt call His name *Jesus.*' Respecting the propriety of that name; the name of Jesus or Joshua, when interpreted, signifying 'God our Saviour' (see Numbers xiii. 16), and so describing with marked exactness what this coming Child was to be, viz., to be One who should 'save His people' (see Jeremiah xxxi. 33–end) 'from their sins.'

Corresponding, moreover, with this voice from heaven, there had been other like voices before.

The well-known prediction of Isaiah vii. 14, for example, had declared that 'a virgin should bring forth a son.'

The angel had now virtually declared the same by explaining the manner in which this wonder was to come true.

The same prophet, in the same place, had declared

that this child of a virgin should bear the name of Emmanuel, or 'God with us.'

The angel has now shewn that this name of 'Jesus' is a perfect fulfilment of this. If God 'saves us,' He must be 'with us' as well. If the child is 'Jesus,' He is 'Emmanuel' too.

Exactly as the angel and the prophecy had described and directed beforehand, so, in every respect, it afterwards comes to pass. 'Joseph, being raised from sleep,' does 'as the angel of the Lord had bidden him, and' takes 'unto him his wife.' Under his holy guardianship she brings forth her 'first-born son;' and to that son, according to the angel's commandment, this name of 'Jesus' is given.

How vividly, therefore, we see this Son of Mary pointed out again as the Christ!

So foretold; so begotten; so named; who else can He be?

CHAPTER III.

HIS PROPER RANK.

Matt. ii.

THE promise to David that the Messiah should sit on his throne, meant more than this a great deal. In fact, when occupied by Messiah, the throne of David was to be the throne of the world. This is clear, amongst other passages, from such as the following :—' All kings shall fall down before Him; all nations shall serve Him,' Ps. lxxii. 11. 'Ask of Me, and I shall give Thee the heathen for Thine inheritance, and the uttermost parts of the earth for Thy possession,' Ps. ii. 8. In that portion of the Evangelist's story (Matt. ii.) to be discussed by us now, this acknowledged item in the national creed must be specially borne in mind.

The 'Virgin's Son' is still an infant when certain 'wise men from the East' arrive at 'Jerusalem.' Their errand is one which takes for granted that the expected King has appeared. Where they can find Him, and how they can worship Him, is all they inquire. Nor do they inquire without cause. The descendants of men who, in all probability, had studied the constellations of heaven for ages, they have seen that in the sky which they regard as an evidence that this 'Star of Jacob' has come. 'Where is He that is born King of the Jews? For we have seen His star in the East, and are come to worship Him.' What profound conviction, to bring them thus far! How true a King, born sceptre-in-hand, as it were! How wide a kingdom, extending even to them!

The inquiry stirs Jerusalem to its centre. The heads of the Church are gathered and questioned by the then head of the state. 'Where is the Christ to be born?' They have but one answer to give. Ancient prophecy had, long ago, settled this point. Out of royal 'Bethlehem,' David's city, David's heir must arise.

On this information Herod immediately acts. Calling the 'wise men' to him in private, he inquires from them with anxious exactness respecting the star they had seen. Then he sends them to Bethlehem to find out with equal exactness the place of the Child, and report it to him. 'In order,' he adds, 'that I may come and worship Him too.'

The wise men 'hear the king,' and depart. To their exceeding joy, the star which they had seen previously befriends them again; guiding them till it stands over where the young Child is. At length they see the Babe! They see its mother! They see the 'King' they desire. Opening the 'treasures' which they have brought so far, they offer Him 'gifts.' The Evangelist specifies what these are. There is the tribute of 'gold,' as befitted a king. There is the fragrance of 'frankincense,' as employed in the worship of God.

There is the virtue of 'myrrh,' as made use of in embalming the dead. Is there unintended prophecy as well as open homage in the choice of these gifts?

Certain it is that deadly designs are already abroad. It is one token of this, that God makes use of a dream to send the 'wise men' home by a different route. It is another token of it that He uses the same instrumentality to protect 'the young Child.' 'The Angel of the Lord' appears to Joseph again. Again, also, is his language urgent, his instructions definite, his reasons precise. 'Arise, and take the young Child and His mother, and flee into Egypt, and be thou there until I bring thee word; for Herod will seek the young Child to destroy Him.'

Thus admonished, 'he arises and takes the young Child and His mother'—not impossibly the same 'night'—into Egypt.

The Evangelist here refers again to the prophetical word. Often, when inspiration speaks of Israel, it means Israel's Messiah as well. There is a passage in Hosea (ch. xi. 1) in which Jehovah is represented as saying: 'Out of Egypt have I called My Son.' In the Evangelist's view, this was a passage in point. It was a 'declaration spoken of the Lord,' according to him—a declaration, therefore—here he anticipates a little—which was 'fulfilled' in His case.

What is next related illustrates this alleged identity of experience between Israel's Messiah and Israel itself, in a very terrible way. Finding that the wise men do not return to him with the information he desires, Herod is greatly enraged; and turns, in consequence, to seek the object which he had really been aiming at all along, in a different way. The priests had informed him of the proper birth-place, the wise men had enabled him to compute the probable age, of the infantile Christ. He will employ this knowledge to make sure of His death. With characteristic recklessness, all infants whatever in the city of Bethlehem, or anywhere near, of anything like the probable age, are to perish, in hopes that this Infant shall perish among them. So he orders. So it is done.

Something of this, also, generations before, the eyes of prophecy had foreseen. The exceedingly bitter anguish caused by the sudden loss of so many little ones, just at that age when they seem to belong to their mothers more than to any one else, those far-seeing eyes had perceived. They had also perceived the exact locality on which this grievous shadow should fall, viz., on the whole of that neighbourhood which was so near to the well-known sepulchre of Rachel 'in the way' to Bethlehem (Gen. xxxv. 19, 20), that she might be considered, poetically speaking, the sorrowing mother of all. 'In Rama was there a voice heard, lamentation, and weeping, and great mourning, Rachel weeping for her children, and would not be comforted, because they are not.'

The life of the Infant Christ has been preserved. Where is He to be reared? On this point Joseph receives once again instructions from heaven. Some time after arriving in Egypt, he is told in a dream of the death of Herod. In the same dream, he is commanded to 'take the young Child and His mother, and go into the land of Israel.' Coming to its borders in obedience to this command, he hears that 'Archelaus is reigning in Judæa in the room of his father Herod;' and is afraid to proceed. Once more, therefore, in his perplexity, he is 'warned of God in a dream;' the result being that he 'turns aside' or 'retires' into 'the parts of Galilee,' and there finally takes up his abode in 'a city called Nazareth.' In this city, said to be the most despised of all in those much despised 'parts,' the Child Jesus is reared. And thus, as foretold in substance by 'the prophets,' this royal descendant of David and Abraham comes to be 'called a Nazarene.'

The whole chapter, in short, presents Him to us in a similar twofold light. Everywhere in it we find evidence that He is 'King of the Jews,' and all that that means. The star in the East, the wise men's journey, the false king's inquiries, the priests' reply, the wise men's offerings, the subsequent plots and massacre, these repeated dreams, these numerous prophecies, these singular providences, all testify to this truth. Yet everywhere, also, He is presented to us as a King in disguise. It is not difficult to see why. He has come to 'minister;' and not, at present, to 'reign.'

PART III.

THE MINISTRY OF CHRIST.

CHAPTER I.

ITS SOLEMN OPENING.

Matt. iii.

WE left 'Jesus of Nazareth' growing up as a child in that city of evil repute. Another figure has to pass before us before we see Him again.

It is the figure of one who is unusually distinguished as a preacher of truth.

He is distinguished by the fact of his preaching out 'in the wilderness,' away from the habitations of men.

He is distinguished by his requiring those who receive his teaching to receive baptism from him as well:—so much so as to have become universally known, in consequence, as 'John the Baptist.'

He is distinguished, further, by the unexampled urgency of his exhortations and message. Others had spoken of a 'kingdom of God' in the future. He proclaims it 'at hand.'

More than this, he even announces himself to expectant Israel as that immediate forerunner of this heavenly kingdom who had been long ago promised as a 'voice in the wilderness' by the prophet Isaiah— their greatest prophet in word.

Further, he is clad and nurtured in such a manner

as inevitably to suggest a comparison with that strangely-fed mantle-clad 'Elijah the Tishbite,' who had been their greatest prophet in deed; and who had also been spoken of as to come immediately 'before the day of the Lord.'

At the same time, he surpasses both those great ones in the results of his work. 'Jerusalem, and all Judæa, and all the region round about Jordan,' not only come to his preaching, but obey his injunctions; and that, also, notwithstanding the deep and open humiliation which such obedience involved. They are 'baptized of him in Jordan, confessing their sins.'

Lastly, this extraordinary popularity is never attributable to his speaking lightly of evil. Amongst those who 'come to his baptism' are many members of the leading sects of the day. He treats them as he treats all, without favour or fear. It is an astonishment to him to find such as they shewing even this token for good. 'O generation of vipers, who hath warned you to flee from the wrath to come?' He warns them, therefore, even with more than wonted earnestness, to be truly sincere in their doings; and to avoid anxiously that formal hypocrisy by which they were deluding their souls. 'Think not to say within yourselves, We have Abraham to our father: for I say unto you, that God is able of these stones to raise up children unto Abraham.' .

Never, surely, did any preacher employ greater boldness of speech.

Never, at the same time, did any preacher labour with more signal success.

Yet, after all, we find him describing it, as his principal work as a teacher to tell men of another. According to his own account, in fact, this is why he has come; and why he acts as he does.

This, for example, is why he is so especially urgent in demanding true repentance of life. That great Searcher of hearts, who is so close behind him, will make short work of anything less. Already, as it were, He is laying His axe at the root of the tree. The next thing, therefore—with every fruitless tree—will be to hew it down for the fire.

This, also, is why this most successful of preachers insists on baptism as he does. Not so much for its own sake, as for what it prepares for, does he make use of this sign. One is coming who is so much mightier than himself that he feels unworthy to do Him service even in the lowliest way. My baptism is 'with water unto repentance.' Its principal use, therefore, is to prepare you for His, which shall be 'with the Holy Ghost, and with fire.'

It is not possible for me, in short, to speak too highly—so he proceeds in effect—either of Him or His work. What an instrument of discrimination, e.g., is that 'fan' of 'His' which He now holds 'in His hand!' How 'throughly' may He be expected, by its help, to 'purge' 'His' own 'floor!' And how wide apart and how irrevocable, therefore, will be the separation it works! Where is the 'wheat?' In the 'garner.' Where is the 'chaff?' In the 'fire.' What sort of 'fire?' That which cannot be 'quenched.'

As John is engaged in teaching thus, Jesus of Nazareth appears before us again. He has left the place and condition of childhood; He arrives at that part of the Jordan where John is baptizing; He applies for baptism at his hands.

The request comes upon that faithful teacher as an utter surprise: not to say, at first, as a shock. So much so, that instead of being ready to administer baptism in this case, he desires to 'forbid' it. The very idea seems to him to set everything wrong. 'I have need to be baptized of Thee; and comest Thou to me?'

Evidently he appears to see in this Jesus that mightier One of whom he has spoken.

The answer of Jesus, though very gracious, is also very decisive. I ask you, as things are 'now,' to 'suffer' this to take place. It is in most admirable keeping, though it may not seem so at first, with the work which I am now to begin. The very purpose I have come for is that of occupying the place of the unrighteous, and 'fulfilling all righteousness' in his stead.

It speaks much, as well both for the knowledge as for the faith of John the Baptist, that he is convinced by this answer, and opposes no longer. Jesus is baptized with "the baptism of repentance unto the remission of sins!"

The baptism over, He 'goeth up straightway out of the water.'

The seal of-approbation is set immediately on that which Jesus has done.

From the opened heavens above the Spirit of God is seen coming down in dove-like fashion and alighting on Jesus.

From the same heavens a Voice is heard which testifies thus:—'This is My beloved Son, in whom I am well pleased.'

See in all this, therefore, how this Jesus of Nazareth is set apart for His ministry!

How singularly great is that preacher of righteousness who sets Him apart!

How evidently and vastly greater is Jesus Himself!

How unexpected, yet how profoundly adequate, is His own view of His work.

How Divinely attested His call!

CHAPTER II.

ITS SUPREME IMPORTANCE.

Matt. iv. 1-11.

AFTER Jesus has been set apart, we find Him setting out, for His work. He does not decide about it alone. That same Eternal Spirit who had just designated and anointed Him for His office, now directs its discharge. The very first step in His Ministry is determined in this manner. 'Then is Jesus led up of the Spirit.' How marked is the solemnity of this statement!

That first step, however, appears at first sight to be most unexpected and strange. Where is Jesus led from? Where to? He is led away from the society and even from the sight of mankind. He is led to a region in which He will have to face the assaults of the great Adversary of mankind. This is described, indeed, as the express purpose for which He is brought to that place. 'Then is Jesus led up of the Spirit into the wilderness, to be tempted of the devil.' Scarcely is His ministry open before we hear the sounds of contention and battle.

Some considerable time, however, seems to elapse before the chief assaults are delivered. Nearly six weeks of solitude and privation pass over this Son of God without producing much sensible effect on His bodily frame. Other men have experienced something not altogether dissimilar when exposed to great and unusual excitement. Amongst the things which the extraordinary measure of this experience in the case of Jesus of Nazareth may serve to shew us, is the extraordinary intensity of feeling with which He opened His work. That work to Him, from the very first, is more than His necessary food.

When the feeling of hunger, and of consequent bodily weakness, comes on Him at last, there comes also the foremost of the expected assaults. Wonderful is the amount of skill with which it seems to be planned. This fainting Man is assailed by a temptation just suited to His condition, the temptation of a prospect of food. It is a temptation, also, exactly suited to the holy simplicity of His character. It sets before Him no greater luxury than a prospect of 'bread.' Also, the temptation comes to Him in a shape nicely adjusted to the dignity of His claims. 'A voice from heaven, only the other day, proclaimed Thee God's Son. Is the Son of God to suffer hunger like the children of men? If Thou hast the power, why not exert the power, and bid these stones become bread?'

The answer to this intricate and subtle temptation is alike sufficient and simple. 'Although in truth the Son of God, I am here as a man; and "man" has been appointed, and has also been taught, to live in entire dependence upon God.'

One avenue of temptation is closed. The act of closing it opens another. 'Dost Thou depend upon God? Then depend on Him to the full. See, here is His House! Here its loftiest point! Are not His angels about Thee? Are they not all charged to preserve Thee? To preserve Thy feet even from coming in contact with the very stones in Thy path? Shew Thy faith in this promise—shew Thy faith in their care—shew Thy faith in Thyself—by flinging Thyself down from this height.'

One ray of truth clears away all this mist of deceit. 'It is forbidden to any man thus to test the limits of God's sovereign will.'

The Saviour has been twice tempted as the Son of God; and has answered as man. He shall now be tempted as man. Taken to the summit of an 'exceeding high mountain,' He is shewn a sudden and far-reaching prospect of 'all the kingdoms of the world.' All the 'glory' that has ever dazzled the longing thoughts of the most ambitious of men lies spread at His feet. If He will only do homage to its present possessor it shall all become His. 'All these things will I give Thee, if Thou wilt fall down and worship me.' What a prospect! What a condition! Never before had so dazzling a result been offered in return for so apparently simple an act!

Not for a single moment, however, was it so regarded by the Man invited thereto. The other temptations had come, as it were, disguised by a cloak. This is a naked incentive to evil. It is a direct incentive to treason against the Most High. Unlike the other temptations, therefore, it meets at once with a direct and naked rebuke. 'Get thee hence, thou Adversary; for it is written, Thou shalt worship the Lord thy God, and Him only shalt thou serve.'

Then, at last, the Evil One goes. Who come in his place? A company of angels from heaven. That arch-deceiver had spoken strict truth when he spoke of them as engaged on Christ's side. They supply His needs. They sustain His faintness. They sympathize with His work. Having come Himself for the purpose of ministering unto many, they minister now unto Him.

See, therefore, how important a thing in every way His Ministry is. The Spirit of God Himself directs it from the first. The whole humanity of Christ Himself is absorbed in it from the first. The mightiest potentate of hell from beneath, with the subtlest of temptations and the costliest of bribes, sets himself in action against it. Afterwards the inhabitants of heaven come down to assist in it, so far as they can. Everywhere it is watched—this blind earth alone excepted—with the deepest concern!

CHAPTER III.

ITS MARKED UNOBTRUSIVENESS.

Matt. iv. 12-25.

THE appointed conflict with Satan in the wilderness has been fully fought out, and Jesus of Nazareth is found again among the dwellings of men. Where does He fix His abode? This the Evangelist explains next.

In the first instance, however, he seems to do so only in a negative way. The choice of a definite centre of labour does not appear to have been made by the newly-set-apart Prophet of Nazareth, until the public labours of the man who had set Him apart have been brought to a close. Up till then He appears to have spent the time subsequent to the Temptation in some place or places of a comparatively conspicuous description. At any rate, it is not until Jesus 'hears that John is cast into prison,' that we are told of His 'retiring' (ἀνεχώρησεν) into that part of the country where we hear of Him next.

This was that peculiarly provincial province of 'Galilee' where He had been brought up as a child.

It is not, however, to that *city* of Galilee in which He had lived as a child, and in which many of His immediate kinsfolk were resident still, that we find Him directing His steps.

He even seems to turn aside from this city in a manner so marked as to excite surprise, if not wrath.

'Leaving Nazareth,' the Evangelist says, 'He comes and settles in Capernaum, which is on the shore of the sea, and in the borders of Zabulon and Nephthalim.'

Possibly St. Matthew speaks in this manner because himself resident there at that time. The 'coming' of Jesus to that city, and the exact aspect and situation of the city itself, would naturally be much impressed on his mind.

Possibly, also, he speaks thus on account of the remarkable character of this step.

With such a mission, for example, as that which has now been entrusted to Jesus, is it not a step to be noted? After being almost worshipped by so great a preacher as John the Baptist, after receiving the open attestation of Heaven itself, after vanquishing the Adversary himself in the wilderness, who would have thought of His settling down in 'Galilee of the Gentiles,' of all places on earth?

Also, if He must begin in that province, why not do so amongst His own kinsfolk and friends? Why venture as a stranger into the thronged streets of a turbulent seafaring town?

The Evangelist's answer is that this had all been determined on ages before; and had also been determined on then for very good cause. Ages before, in the mystic language of the prophet Isaiah, God had seen fit to reveal how the coming Light of the world should give special enlightenment to that part of the world; and how it should do so (apparently) for the very good reason that the darkness there would be worst. 'The land of Zabulon, and the land of Nephthalim, by the way of the sea, beyond Jordan, Galilee of the Gentiles; the people which sat in darkness saw great light; and to them which sat in the region and shadow of death light is sprung up.'

Having thus selected as His starting-point and head-quarters this appointed centre of darkness, how does Jesus proceed?

First of all, He again takes up the special message of His predecessor, the Baptist. 'From that time Jesus begins to preach, and to say, Repent: for the Kingdom of Heaven is at hand.'

Walking, next, by the neighbouring sea, He influences first one, and then another, amongst the fisherfolk on its waters, as they are casting their nets into the sea, or else mending them after having done so, to give up all for His sake; promising to them, if they will so 'follow' Him, that they shall become 'fishers of men.'

After that, from Capernaum as His centre, but still always within the borders of Galilee as His circumference, He goes everywhere teaching and preaching the glad tidings of the Kingdom of God, at the same time relieving and healing in a perfectly marvellous manner all the manifold ailments and sicknesses of all those who throng to Him for such help.

Finally, as the news of these strange proceedings gradually permeates to all parts of the land, helpless patients in every stage and shape of bodily and mental affliction are brought to Him in such numbers, and are relieved by Him also with such completeness, that He finally finds Himself followed by crowds gathered together, not only from Galilee itself, but also from cities as diverse in character as half-heathen Decapolis and self-righteous Jerusalem, and from places as far remote from one another and from Him as the parts of Judæa beyond Jerusalem and the wide country on the other side of the Jordan.

Thus it is that Jesus commences His direct ministerial work. In after years Christianity is taught to 'begin at Jerusalem,' and is eager of itself to encounter philosophy at Athens, and to face empire at Rome. Christ Himself, at this outset of His labours, deliberately turns from them all. Although the wide and immediate spread of His 'fame' shews plainly what He might have done in the most famous parts of the world, He chooses instead, of set purpose, to begin with the despised and obscure. And He does so, moreover, with no other object than their enlightenment and relief. So full of meekness—so full of mercy—is His ministry from the first!

CHAPTER IV.

ITS UNEXAMPLED AUTHORITY.

Matt. v. vi. vii.

WE have now arrived at that point of our road where its longer stages begin; the 'stations' of this journey, as of many others, lying much thicker together towards its beginning and end.

The precise 'longer stage' at this moment before us, consists of the whole of the three next chapters of our Evangelist's work. We take them together because we find them occupied with one subject throughout. By this time of the Saviour's history, so many persons have begun to attach themselves to Him as His disciples, that He seems to think it necessary to issue to them a kind of MANIFESTO of His teaching. It is this MANIFESTO which is reported to us in the three chapters referred to. 'Seeing the multitudes, He went up into the mountain: and when He was set, His disciples came unto Him; and He opened His mouth, and taught them.'

In the set discourse thus delivered by Him, He first encourages; next enlightens; and finally, cautions His disciples.

He *encourages* them by assuring them repeatedly

of the peculiar blessedness of their lot. He bids them be sure of this, notwithstanding the fact—a fact which would be plain enough to them afterwards, if not quite clear at that time—that all the peculiarities of their lot were not such as would be thought enviable in the eyes of the world. To the world, e. g., it seemed anything but a blessing to be 'poor in spirit,' or 'mournful,' or 'meek;' or to be eager in the pursuit of 'righteousness' instead of the good things of this life; or to be men of 'mercy,' or of inward 'purity,' or effectual promoters of 'peace.' Still less so, to be exposed to suffering or shame 'for righteousness' sake.' Yet in these self-same things, so He deliberately assures them, lay the peculiar felicity of their lot. For, just in proportion as these things were true of them now, so would the exact opposites be true of them hereafter in a simply immeasurable degree. Just in the same proportion, also, would they enjoy in the meantime the God-like privileges of preserving the world as its 'salt,' and blessing the world as its 'light,' and so causing their 'Father in heaven' to be 'glorified' upon earth. Such was the happiness—the unexpected happiness—to which His disciples were called.

The special point on which Jesus next proceeds to *enlighten* His disciples is that of His position as a Teacher.

First, on its negative side. Let them never suppose that He had come for the purpose of in any way depreciating those ancient authorities of the 'Law and the Prophets' to which they had been taught to look up. Rather, He had come for the express purpose of vindicating them to the full. So long, in fact, as heaven and earth themselves should continue in existence, so long also even their minutest portions would continue in force. Neither would any one whatever in the Kingdom of Heaven be able either to practise or teach otherwise, except at the most serious loss to himself. Some there were, it is true, who seemed, even then, to think that they could. Such teachers were not examples, but warnings. *His* disciples must surpass them, if they would even 'enter into the Kingdom of Heaven.'

For Himself, what He taught respecting these rules —to come now to the positive side—was their exceeding penetration and breadth. Previous teachers, in declaring God's will, had published the 'letter' of His witness against sin—a most valuable thing in its way. The prerogative which He assumed was that of proclaiming its 'spirit.'

On the subject of murder, e. g., they 'of old' had been contented with saying, 'Thou shalt not kill.' Jesus taught that the commandment extended even to wishing harm without cause; and that any deliberate manifestation of malicious desire, or avoidable carelessness about causing pain or giving offence, was a transgression which exposed the offender to the severe displeasure of God.

On the subject of impurity, again, they 'of old time' had written down the command, 'Thou shalt not commit adultery.' Jesus teaches His disciples that they must not even desire it; and bids them be ready rather to sacrifice their 'right eye' or 'right hand' than indulge in adulterous thoughts.

So, also, on the important question of the dissolution of marriage. Previous authorities had put the dissolution of this tie on the same serious and formal footing as the contraction thereof. Jesus teaches that neither party must think of dissolving it by legal measures, till the other party has dissolved it in fact.

Once, again, on the subject of swearing they 'of old time' had taught men not to perjure themselves before God. Jesus goes to the root of the matter by teaching men never to use language inconsistent with the recollection of God's infinite greatness and sovereignty, and of man's utter impotence and dependence.

Finally, while previous commandments had taught men never to exact more than equal retaliation for the wrongs they received, Jesus again goes to the root of the matter by reminding men that, as offenders themselves, they have no right in reality to exact retaliation of any description. Instead of this, what really becomes them as sinful creatures, is to imitate their 'Father in heaven' by doing good and shewing kindness both to enemies and to friends.

It is with this same principle, in fact, that He winds

up these new enactments of His respecting the duty of man. 'Be ye therefore perfect, even as your Father which is in heaven is perfect.'

From explaining God's will, Jesus passes to exposing men's thoughts. Special dangers beset those who seriously address themselves—as many of these His professed 'disciples' were undoubtedly doing—to the task of fulfilling that will. How well these dangers were understood by Him is shewn by the series of *Cautions* with which He concludes.

The first group of these is directed against the great mistake of seeking the praise of men rather than the approval of God. It is, unhappily, natural to all of us to think more of men than of God. Even in matters which have exclusively to do with His worship, such as offering our gifts, and saying our prayers, and humbling our persons in His presence—matters in which the desire of man's appreciation and favour is specially misplaced, and therefore specially injurious also—this danger besets us. How is it to be averted? The plan recommended by Jesus is of the most effectual kind, viz., by cutting off the occasion. If we do not allow other men even to know of what we are doing, the desire of pleasing them will never require to be resisted, for it will never arise.

The next caution is directed against the great mistake of setting our affections on the perishable riches of earth; thereby failing of ever attaining the imperishable riches of heaven. If once we allow ourselves really to 'love' money, we have made it our god. And if once we do this, then, like all other idolators, we shall serve the true God no more. 'Ye cannot serve God *and* Mammon.'

Hence the necessity, as the Master points out next, of being on one's guard against a very much subtler form of the same tyrannical evil. 'Covetousness,' men think, is one thing; 'prudence' is another. Can it ever be wrong for us to labour diligently for fit raiment and food? It is certain to be wrong—so the Master replies in effect—if we labour for them in that spirit of anxiety and distraction which is only another name for trust in self and distrust of God. Such anxiety is unreasonable, to begin. Cannot He sustain the life and clothe the body who brought both into being? In the next place, it is wholly unnecessary. 'The birds of the air' know nothing of it, and yet are abundantly 'fed.' .In the third place, it is utterly vain. The lilies of the field never dream of it, and yet are better clad than ourselves. In the last place, it is specially and doubly injurious to ourselves. By putting the 'kingdom of God' into the second place instead of the first, we miss the very things which we seek; and by anticipating the evils of to-morrow, we add them to those of to-day—which are always great enough as it is. .

The next group of cautions warns the disciples of Christ against dangers which beset them in their intercourse with their fellows. Considering your own liability to self-deception and error, be very careful not to sit in judgment on the mistakes of others until you have disposed of your own. On the other hand, be equally careful not to waste your treasures or risk your safety by pressing truth upon men who are avowedly wedded to defilement, like so many 'dogs,' or only capable of appreciating that which is sensual, like so many 'swine.' The wise rule, in all cases, is to bear in mind the more than fatherly readiness of God in heaven 'to give good things to them that ask Him;' and to be guided thereby. For His sake, always endeavour to do unto others as you would have them do unto you. This is My rule. This is the old rule. There is no better rule to be found.

The last group of cautions is a kind of application of all that precedes.

Beware of being carried away, with regard to error and truth, by the mere suffrages of mankind. The way of the multitude is not the way, either of safety or truth, as a rule.

Beware, also, of being carried away by the mere professions of men. Only those can be trusted to teach truth who have truly learned to do good.

Beware, above all things, of allowing yourselves to be satisfied with the mere knowledge of truth. No stability is like the stability of the disciple who understands and obeys. Such a man builds on a 'rock.' On the other hand, there is no overthrow like the overthrow of the deceiver who hears and does not.

Such a man builds on the 'sand.' The higher he builds, therefore, the more irretrievable is the final crash of his house.

These, very briefly, are the principal features of this set and solemn discourse. In still briefer retrospect, we see now how much they imply. What authority in blessing! What authority in legislation! What wisdom in warning! Everything that His manner claims—however much—His matter sustains. The multitudes hear and are astounded. 'He spake as one having authority,' and not merely as one claiming it, as was the case with 'the Scribes.' Never before had they listened to any one so 'mighty in word!'

CHAPTER V.

ITS UNRIVALLED POWER.

Matt. viii. ix. 1-35.

WITH the exception of two separate portions of a few verses each, the whole of the next chapter of this Gospel, and the whole also of the first thirty-five verses of the following chapter, are taken up with a detailed narrative of certain doings of Christ. This is not unnatural after the special attention just paid to His sayings. These same 'sayings' teach the necessity of comparing a teacher's words with his works.

Very instructive, in this light, is the first of these 'doings.' As soon as Jesus comes down from the mountain, a poor outcast, afflicted with leprosy, flings himself at His feet. In all the previous history of the chosen people, only two instances of the cure of this terrible malady are on record. Their sacred law itself, with its many minute and comprehensive directions on other points, gave none upon this. All it did was to shew the sufferer how to conduct himself, if relieved. How great, therefore, is the confidence of this sufferer in the healing power of Jesus of Nazareth, to make him cry out as he does:—'Sir, if Thou art willing, Thou art able, to cleanse me.'

How great also is the confidence of Jesus in Himself, when He first touches, and then replies to him, 'I am willing: be thou cleansed.' Nor was this confidence vain. The thing is no sooner spoken than done. The man's leprosy is gone. His uncleanness is cleansed. Jesus is more than he thought.

After this, Jesus returns to Capernaum. He meets, as He enters, with a yet greater example of confidence in His power. A Roman centurion approaches Him with an earnest request. A cruel disease, which even modern science finds peculiarly insusceptible of remedial treatment, has laid its hand with peculiar severity on one attached to his house. 'My servant lieth at home sick of the palsy, grievously tormented.' With the same confidence as in the previous instance, Jesus replies immediately: 'I will come and heal him.' To this the centurion, most unexpectedly, replies again, in effect: 'Not so, sir, for I am not worthy that Thou shouldest come to my house. Only give Thou the word of command to this sickness, as I do to the soldiers under me, and it will be as sure to obey.' Jesus Himself marvels at such pre-eminent faith in an outsider. And He meets it at once, therefore, if so we may say, by a like pre-eminent boon. All that the centurion has asked for, the helpless anguish of his distant servant receives, 'in that self-same hour.'

Coming, after this, into 'Peter's house,' Jesus finds that disciple's 'wife's mother' prostrated by 'fever.' He touches her hand; the fever is gone, and all its after effects. Instead of being waited on, she is able to wait upon them.

Before the end of that day, multitudes in this city of Capernaum have heard of these cures, and bring their afflicted ones to His presence. Jesus is equal to all. With a mysterious depth and intimacy of sympathy, foreseen and admired afar off in the pages of prophecy, He takes the burdens of all on Himself. All, in consequence, are relieved. The very 'devils' come out, the worst 'infirmities' vanish, by the mere force of His word.

There is danger lest the continually increasing excitement aroused by this succession of marvels should become a hindrance rather than a help to Christ's work as a Teacher. Possibly this is why, 'when He sees great multitudes about Him, He gives commandment to depart unto the other side.' This also may be the reason why He warns a certain stranger who chooses this time for openly offering to follow Him 'whithersoever He goeth,' of the heavy cost of so doing. 'The foxes have holes, and the birds of the air have nests; but the Son of Man hath not where to lay His head.' And this may be, finally, why He now teaches another, who calls himself a 'disciple' already, that the cost of discipleship, however heavy, must be fully discharged. 'Follow Me; and let the dead bury their dead.' Jesus has no wish to be surrounded by idle admirers of the mere manifestation of power.

The case is altered, however, when He has left the crowds of Capernaum behind Him, and is out on the sea, in the believing company of His chosen disciples alone. It is good for them to have their faith established by further proof of His power. First, however, that faith is tried by a storm. Heavy seas cover the vessel. Death seems unavoidable, unless they are delivered by Him. Can He deliver them, lying asleep? Judging from the touch of rudeness, if not of despair, which marks their appeal to Him, they seem to think not. 'Lord, save us; we are being lost!' How does Jesus reply? First, He rebukes, but in the gentlest manner, the feebleness of their faith. 'Why are ye fearful, O ye of little faith?' Then He 'rebukes,' having risen up, 'the winds and the sea.' Immediately, much as in the previous case of the fever, not only do the winds cease, but the effects of them too. The heaving waters become as calm as though they had never been stirred, and there falls also on the disciples themselves a similar awe. 'What manner of man is this, that even the winds and the sea obey Him!'

Meanwhile, a worse kind of tempest is raging on land. As Jesus and His disciples disembark in the country of the Gergesenes, they are met by its victims. Two demoniacs, so exceeding fierce that no one might pass by that way, come down to the shore. They have come to supplicate, however, not to attack. The malignant spirits who have possession of their faculties cry out by their lips, 'What have we to do with Thee, Jesus, Thou Son of God? Art Thou come hither to torment us before the time? If Thou dost cast us out, wilt Thou not at least permit us some other refuge? May we not enter those swine?' Jesus says to them, 'Go.' They come out, accordingly, and enter the swine, which are to be seen feeding on the mountain side a good way off by the shore of the lake. In a moment there is a sudden downward frantic rush of all the unclean beasts into the waters of the sea. The next moment there is an almost equally sudden and terrified flight of all the swineherds to tell the tidings at home. Before long all the inhabitants of the city are seen coming out to meet Christ. They do meet Him, but only to entreat Him that they may see Him no more. Such is the homage—the terrified homage—which they pay to His power.

Back again in 'His own city,' we read of further wonderful deeds. The first of these is in direct connection with the peculiar dignity of His claims. Certain persons bring unto Him a poor man so afflicted with palsy that he can only lie helplessly on his bed. 'Seeing their faith,' Jesus at once directs His mercy to the deepest need of their friend. 'Son, be of good cheer; thy sins be forgiven thee.' To some there, such language has a simply blasphemous sound. Jesus, therefore, replies next to their thoughts. He justifies His words by His actions. By manifestly remitting part of the consequences of sin, He shews His right to assure men of the remission of its guilt. The man had been brought there as a burden. Jesus bids him take up the bed he had been brought on, and himself carry it home. The multitude see him do so; and, with just discrimination, glorify God for giving such 'authority' unto men.

We read next of the calling of Matthew himself, while engaged in his work as a tax-gatherer or 'publican;' of certain difficulties which seem to have arisen in consequence between the Pharisees and the disciples of Christ; and of certain other not very dissimilar difficulties between His disciples and the disciples of John the Baptist. Postponing the consideration of these topics till they come before us again (as they speedily will), we come upon a miracle next, in which the amazing power of Jesus is manifested in a wholly new sphere. A certain 'ruler' asks Him, in effect, to restore life to the dead. 'My daughter is even now dead; but come and lay Thy hand upon her, and she shall live.' The Saviour arises without demur, and proceeds towards the man's house. The disciples go with Him too. Whilst on His way, there comes another appeal—a kind of parenthetical appeal—to His power. A poor woman, who has suffered for twelve weary years from an issue of blood, comes behind Him in the press. 'If I may but touch the hem of His garment,' she says to herself, 'it will do.' The appeal of that touch, though but a mute one, reaches His heart. Turning Him about in the fulness of His mercy and power, He blesses and restores her both in body and soul ; and then proceeds to the house of the dead. There He finds all the usual evidences of the presence of death. So much so, that when He gives expression to certain mysterious words of consolation and hope, which imply a continuance of life in this case, they are received with derision and scorn. There, nevertheless, by the touch of His hand, these words are justified to the full. Death itself, in His presence, is found to be only a 'sleep.' She who had certainly died is alive again, and the land is alive with the news.

Two blind men—not blind in mind—come to Him next. 'Jesus, Thou Son of David'—so they cry as they follow His footsteps—' have mercy upon us.' Before He relieves them, they must confess openly their faith in His power. ' Believe ye that I am able to do this?' They say unto Him : ' Yea, Lord ;' and He touches their eyes. With the touch their sight is restored. With the restoration comes the injunction—the wellnigh severe injunction, as the word seems to signify—not to tell other men of this deed. As before, Jesus shrinks from the very suspicion of making a display of His power.

The blind men, notwithstanding this injunction, depart open-mouthed. Then a dumb man is brought in. A certain cruel Satanic power lies at the root of his silence. But when Jesus speaks, he is compelled to speak too. Hearing this, the multitudes, in turn, speak their unbounded surprise. ' It was never so seen in Israel.' Last of all, even unbelief itself, in its unwilling fashion, confesses as much. 'He casteth out devils,' the Pharisees say, 'through the prince of the devils.' This is the voice, in reality, of despair. No one offers so suicidal a solution who has anything better to urge.

After all, however, in this constellation of wonders, we have only a sample, as it were, of this sky. Everywhere and everywhen else, at this time, whithersoever Jesus goes—so the Evangelist tells us next—similar miracles are repeated. It is not necessary that he should give these in detail after what he has done. The reason why he details the others, in all probability, is because they came to pass in Capernaum about the time of his own call to discipleship; and so, not impossibly, had much to do with fixing his attention on, and confirming his faith in, the mission of Christ. Anyhow, looked upon as specimens of His doings, what a picture of power they present. We saw before that He was 'mighty in word.' These shew that He is also 'mighty in deed.' If He speaks with authority, He acts with power. Nothing is beyond His easy control. He has power over sickness, whatever its nature. Power over the elements, whatever their condition. Power over devils, however malignant and many. Power over death, however complete its control. Last of all, and most of all— if so we may venture to express ourselves—power over Himself. Everything required for the success of His mission, or for the relief of suffering humanity, is vouchsafed by Him without stint. Nothing is done, nothing is encouraged—everything rather is strictly forbidden—which would merely magnify His personal fame. Even the 'last infirmity of noble minds' is banished from His!

CHAPTER VI.

ITS FEW HELPS.

Matt. ix. 36-38, x.

TWICE before, in this narrative, has special mention been made of the 'multitudes' about Christ. In the first instance (ch. v. 1), the sight led to the promulgation of that special code of instruction, the Sermon on the Mount. In the second instance (ch. viii. 18), the sight induced Him—probably, as we saw, with the view of avoiding misconception and hindrance—to 'give commandment to depart to the other side.' A third result, different from either, is described to us now. This time the spectacle fills Him with a mingled feeling of compassion and want; of compassion, when He thinks of the necessities of the multitude; of want, when He remembers His own. As the sheep of His pasture, 'scattered' and ready to 'faint,' they require to be gathered together and fed. As claiming Himself to be a greater and truer shepherd than any before, what He requires now is a supply of under-shepherds to assist in His work. In other words, as He next puts it Himself, what He specially needs now is a supply of reapers for the in-gathering of the 'harvest.' This is the difficulty which the very success of His ministry has brought into being. A 'harvest' of souls, ready for reaping, is standing all round. A supply of 'labourers,' ready to reap it, does not at present exist. The one is 'plenteous;' the others are 'few.'

In this state of things it is specially the duty of all His true disciples to join together in prayer. Prayer is a proper refuge in all emergencies. It is specially proper in this. In providing labourers for 'His harvest,' who so willing to hear, who so likely to answer, and who so able, if need be, even to constrain men to give their assistance, as 'the Lord of the harvest Himself?' This, therefore, is the first thing to be done. Do 'ye,' My disciples, see to it, that ye do not fail on this point.

But, if prayer is first, action is next. The Lord Jesus, accordingly, proceeds next to an important first step in this line. He solemnly sets apart a certain number of chosen disciples to be 'sent out' in His name; and to bear, in consequence, the name of 'Apostles,' i.e. of persons 'sent forth.' The helpers thus selected, however, are only twelve in number, all told, and including among them even that one who afterwards turned out to be false. Neither have any among them any appearance of being persons of station or mark. Four of them we have already heard of as being originally fishermen by occupation, a fact which certainly would not be any special recommendation to them in going forth as Apostles. Another of them we have also heard of already as being originally a 'publican,' a fact which would undoubtedly be greatly against him in almost every one's eyes. Altogether, therefore, the men chosen to be Apostles of Christ do not appear to have been in any way a distinguished set, until thus distinguished by Him.

We find, also, that they are only sent out at first to a strictly limited field. Into the wide 'way of the Gentiles,' and even into the neighbouring 'cities of the Samaritans,' their feet are expressly forbidden to travel. All these, in fact, they are to leave on one side, in order entirely to concentrate their attention on 'Israel's' perishing 'sheep.' Also, even in Israel itself, they are always to labour in entire dependence on the message which they have to deliver, and on Him who has commissioned them to deliver it. In other respects, their only riches are to be the miraculous gifts with which He promises so freely to endow them; their only provision the fatherly succour with which He Himself will assist them; and their only protection the ultimate blessings or judgments which He will send on those who shall either honour or despise their commission. In themselves these Apostles will be as utterly defenceless as so many 'sheep among wolves.' The wisest of creatures, in short, cannot be wiser, neither can the most innocent of creatures be more harmless, than ought to be the case about them. Neither can they again, as a rule, be too suspicious of 'men.' Jewish 'councils' and 'synagogues,' on the one hand, and Gentile 'kings and governors,' on the other, will agree in hating them for His sake. It is true, indeed, that, in endeavouring to testify for Christ in these difficult circumstances, they may reckon on an amount of assistance from above which shall be as effectual as though the Spirit of their Father had spoken for them Himself. But, except on this side, on no other side, must they look for succour or love. 'All men' will hate them; those men the most who ought to love them the most. All men, moreover, will hate them with a degree of hatred against which there is no resource except flight; and to which, also, there will be no termination till the Son of Man has returned. Hating and reviling Christ Himself, in a word, men, as a rule, will revile and persecute to the end, for His sake, all those that are His.

Even so, however, His Apostles must not allow themselves to be frightened away from their task. After all, they will only be teaching that which ought to be taught, and which must come to light in the end. Meantime, there is a very definite natural limit, and also a very carefully defined providential limit, to the amount of evil which their direst enemies will be able to inflict. On the other hand, there is hardly any limit to the amount of providential care which will be exercised on their account—including, if need be, the very 'numbering of their hairs'—if they only confess Christ as they ought. Let them determine, therefore, to face boldly all the evils of which He has told them before, and which He now repeats to them again. Their doing so will prove them indeed to be His. And to be His indeed is to attain —whatever else may betide, and whatever else may be lost—the true end of their lives. For what was Christ their Master Himself, but One 'sent forth' to do good? And what will they be in turn, if this be true about them, but men 'sent forth' in like manner? Men, therefore, destined to become the source of innumerable blessings to all who receive them as such? They may judge of this by one fact. Even so cheap a token of sympathy as the giving of 'a cup of cold water' to one of these 'little ones' in his Master's name cannot possibly lose its reward. So great is the dignity of being a disciple—how much greater, therefore, that of being an apostle—of such a Master as Christ!

These words seem to enshrine the sentiment which is the sum of the whole. What a Master is Christ! No master rewards, no master assists with such bounty as He. The men addressed by Him here are all the helpers of which this Gospel informs us. We see what helpers they are. How few in number! How feeble in power! Think of describing a company of shepherds as 'sheep among wolves!' It is Jesus, in reality, who helps His Apostles; not they who help Him. So singularly solitary is His ministerial work! So far is He, throughout, from being in any way dependent on others. His chosen helpers turn out, in reality, to be the men He helps most!

CHAPTER VII.

ITS MANY OPPONENTS.

Matt. xi. xii.

AFTER the helpers, such as they are, we come to the opponents of Christ. The same outward success which suggested the calling of the former, provoked the animosity of the latter. We find accordingly, in the two next chapters of our Evangelist's story, that he dwells much on this point. Almost all, indeed, that he tells us here on other subjects may be, as it were, threaded on this.

This is true, for example, in what he has now to tell us of that 'John the Baptist' of whom he spoke so honourably before. Although still in prison, as when we heard of him last (ch. iv. 12), the growing fame of Jesus of Nazareth has come to his ears. If he himself hears of this fame without jealousy, it would appear that some of his disciples do not. Once before (Matt. ix. 14), we heard of some of them disputing with the disciples of Christ on a matter of outward observance, but they appear by this time, in some way, to have become further 'offended in' Christ. Either, therefore, for his own comfort, or else for their edification, John sends two of them to ask Jesus the following question:—'Art Thou He that should come; or do we look for another?' What an inquiry from the lips of the man who had come to 'make ready' His 'way!' Is this all that the teaching and example of this John the Baptist have effected thus far? To think that it should be necessary to prove to the disciples of 'John' who 'Jesus of Nazareth' is!

Moreover, this is not by any means a case by itself; as is shewn, next, by that to which this inquiry led up. Notwithstanding the disappointing character of John's inquiry, he was a truly great man. Jesus insists much upon this. From a spiritual point of view, indeed, He declares plainly that no greater one had preceded him. The last, as it were, of the Old dispensation; he was also its glory and crown; and only inferior, in fact, to the New. Yet see how dimly his testimony to Christ has been understood even by those who had professed to receive it! How plain it is, also, that it had been rejected entirely by the greater part of his hearers! They had even rejected in a similar manner the testimony of Jesus Himself. Altogether perverse, indeed, as to the teaching of both of them, had been the conduct of that 'generation.' The forerunner of Christ, in his holy severity, they had pronounced a demoniac! The Christ Himself, in His condescending innocence, they have accused of excess! What a condition of things! After all the teaching, both of Jesus and John, the mass of their hearers are unbelievers in both! Not a few of them their blasphemers as well!

What makes this more serious is another feature, of which Jesus speaks next. There were certain cities in which His teaching might have been expected to meet with signal success. If the many miracles, by which He had heralded and supported that teaching in Chorazin and Bethsaida and Capernaum, had been witnessed in the wealthy Gentile cities of Tyre and Sidon, or even in licentious Sodom itself, this would undoubtedly have been the case. How different the result in these favoured cities of Galilee, considered as a whole! Conspicuous for evidence, they have been equally conspicuous for resisting it too! What an illustration of the deadly nature of the hindrances to His work! Just there, where His works have been the most marvellous, has the resistance to them, if we may say so, been more marvellous still!

The thought leads Him to give utterance to an accurate estimate of the whole of His work. The 'wise and prudent,' the great and prosperous, will not believe in Him, as a rule. In a certain sense, they will be unable to do so on these very accounts. It was not God's will, as it were, that eyes so self-blinded should be capable of seeing the light. That being so, He, for His part, is more than contented—He is even thankful—that so it should be. Must He expect only to labour successfully amongst the 'babes' and the poor? Will none but the 'weary and heavy-laden' in lot—will none but the 'meek and lowly in spirit'—be content to 'learn' at His mouth? He will be more than content, on His part, to address Himself specially to such souls. 'Come unto Me, and I will give rest to you'—so He cries out to them—however others refuse it. 'Take My yoke upon you, and learn of Me, and ye shall find rest to your souls.'

About that 'same time' there took place an occurrence which gave much additional point to these sayings. One Sabbath day the disciples were passing with Jesus through the fields of ripe corn. Being hungry, and seeing the corn, they 'begin to pluck the ears, and to eat.' Hardly have they begun, however, before, much to their scandal, some of the Pharisees 'see it.' The profound opposition of thought which separated Him and them, was immediately brought to light by the sight. They strongly reprehended, and He as fully defended, what His disciples had done. David himself, in principle, long before, had done a precisely similar thing. Their own temple priests, also, in discharging their duties, were constantly incurring similar blame—that is, in reality, none at all. Had they only known, indeed, who was meant by the Temple, and who was the true 'Lord of the Sabbath,' and for what great ultimate purpose all rites were appointed, they would never have been guilty of thus attaching blame to those who were deserving of none. But, as things are now, where is the likelihood of their accepting truth from His lips? That which, with Him, is but a means at the best, they idolise as an end.

This hopeless diversity is still more accentuated very soon after, if not on the very same day. Jesus 'departs thence,' it is said, and goes into 'their' synagogue. There He finds a 'man' with a 'withered hand.' They seek at once, from their point of view, to make use of his case. 'If we suggest to this Jesus to heal this sufferer, He will be sure to do it, even this Sabbath day; and His doing so will at once enable us to accuse Him as an offender.' To a certain extent their manœuvre succeeded. Jesus, while more than justifying Himself by what was constantly done by themselves, heals the man's hand, as expected. Immediately they go out and gather a council, in order thereby to 'destroy Him.' And that with so much eagerness, that, when Jesus 'hears' of it, He 'withdraws' from that place. He knows to what cruel lengths some of His opponents are ready to go.

Not, however, that this leads Him for a moment to forego His labours of love. On the contrary, it is expressly recorded respecting the 'great multitudes' which follow Him in His retirement, that He 'heals them all.' The only thing He insists on is, that they shall 'not make Him known.' This was partly, it may be, because of possible danger, under the circumstances, to Himself; but still more, it seems certain, because of probable consequent injury to His ministry; and because nothing, in fact, could be less in accordance with the predicted unobtrusiveness and mercifulness of its spirit. In the case, however, of one peculiarly notable miracle wrought by Him at that time—a miracle in which a certain blind and dumb demoniac is enabled both to see and to speak—neither the fact itself nor its significance admits of being concealed. The people, therefore, on the one hand, say, Who is this but the son of David? The Pharisees, on the other hand, say, This is Satan divided against himself. A palpable subterfuge which Jesus pronounces to be equally blasphemous and absurd. Nothing, indeed, could well be *more* blasphemous, according to Him. To such awful lengths do some of His opponents now actually go! They approach to the verge, if they do not actually transgress it, of the one unpardonable transgression! We need not wonder that He does not see fit to gratify unbelief such as this with a mere miracle of display: already the men of that generation had seen greater wonders than any generation before. Or that He does see fit, in the end, to retort the charge which they have so daringly brought against Him. True and increasing Satanic assistance and co-operation and possession, there is indeed in this case. Only it is to be found with those who are thus opposed to His merciful labours in that 'wicked generation;' and not with Himself!

'While He yet talks' in this manner, He receives a

message which adds an exceedingly painful finishing touch to this part of His story. Outside the house are standing certain persons who are 'desirous to speak with Him.' They are His nearest relatives upon earth. They have not come, however, in order to hear Him, but in order to interrupt Him in His labours. That this was indeed the purpose of their request, and how deeply, as such, it was felt by Him, His reception of it makes plain. 'My mother and My brethren!' Are these the words ye employed? are they, also, opposed to My work? In that case, I must give their name to others instead. Only those who accept My teaching, none of those who reject My teaching, are true kinsfolk of Mine!

Such is the result, so far, of Christ's message to men. A few among them have really believed. Many times more have disbelieved and despised. Not a few have even come to hate Him as well. In every way the outlook is of the most serious kind. Even amongst those supposed to be 'prepared' for Him, there is the most grievous lack of knowledge and faith. Even where He has laboured the most He seems to have succeeded the least. As for the 'wise and prudent' in the eyes of the world—as for those generally looked up to as authorities on questions of faith—they are none of them on His side. Many of them, on the contrary, are against Him with a degree of subtlety and malignity that seem to be inspired of Satan himself. The very mother that bare Him, at the present moment, is out of sympathy with Him. So doubly solitary is His work upon earth! His friends, as we saw, are very feeble and few; His enemies are correspondingly many and mighty! He has little help, if any, at home; He has every hindrance abroad!

CHAPTER VIII.

ITS SINGULAR WISDOM.

Matt. xiii.

WE have just seen that two principal features mark the position of Christ at this stage. On the one hand, He is surrounded by a few disciples who are in continual need of His help. On the other, He is confronted by many opponents of the most irreconcilable stamp. How can He deal best, in His further teaching, with two such widely differentiated classes of hearers? with this humble dependence? with this implacable pride?

The next portion of St. Matthew's Gospel seems to turn on this point. It begins by telling us of a method of procedure on the part of Christ as a teacher not mentioned before. This method is first adopted 'on the same day' as that on which the wide-spread opposition aroused by His preaching had been made so painfully plain. Leaving the 'house' where He had spoken last on this subject, He takes His seat by the sea. So great multitudes there gather together in order to hear Him, that He finds it necessary to enter into a ship. From that conveniently separated position He addresses these multitudes as they stand on the shore. But all He says to them thus—and

He has much to say—is couched in a shape of its own. 'He speaks many things to them in parables.' We are to understand, evidently, that there is something marked in this change. If ever at all before, certainly never so abundantly before, has He instructed men on this wise.

It is a noteworthy fact that the first of the series of parables introduced to us thus, is one that speaks very largely of labour in vain. So far, indeed, as the outward framework of this well-known 'Parable of the Sower' is concerned, this seems the chief impression produced. At the best, the labour described in it is only a more or less distant approach to success in three cases out of four. It is a true success only in one. In that one case, the labour employed is described as being abundantly fruitful, no doubt—'some thirtyfold, some sixtyfold, some a hundredfold.' But in every other case it is described, in reality, as being entirely fruitless. Is the Saviour still thinking of the many hindrances to His own work when He speaks in this manner? He is certainly referring to that which, in His judgment, deserved attention as much. 'He that hath ears to hear, let him hear.'

The disciples naturally ask the reason of this new manner of speech. 'Why speakest Thou unto them in parables?' The Master's answer points to that very distinction to which we adverted just now. There is a difference, He says, both as to purpose and character, between others and you. You are destined to 'know' these 'mysteries,' which shall be mysteries for ever to them. Even if you are not very wise at this moment, you possess at least the seed of wisdom in being willing to learn. That 'little,' therefore, in your case, shall in time become much. They, on the other hand, possess comparatively 'nothing,' because unwilling to learn. Consequently, that 'nothing' itself, in their case, shall in time be 'taken away.' And why I speak unto them in parables, is because this form of speech is found to accomplish both these two ends at one time. On the one hand, its outward obscurity doubles the darkness of the many eyes that close themselves against truth—just as prophecy said that it would. On the other hand, its inward radiance enlightens beyond anything else the eyes of those who really look for that radiance—as is the happy case with yourselves.

When this particular parable itself comes to be interpreted, it is found to carry on the same thought. Yes, it *was* of Himself that Christ was thinking when He put this parable forth. That 'word of the kingdom' which He was then engaged in preaching was what He meant by the 'seed.' The different soils on which the seed is described as falling, correspond to the different classes of hearers to whom that word was then being addressed. And the varied results which were flowing then from His labours, and the diverse reasons which accounted for them, are what the rest of the parable shews. This, at any rate, it signified at the first. Afterwards, no doubt, just because it signified this at the first, it also signifies more.

'Another parable' is put forth, next, which is also about 'seed.' In the previous one, the evil depicted had been principally of a negative kind. The seed sown, as a rule, had not produced fruit. In the present parable we hear of evil in a more positive form. We hear of direct efforts in opposition to the man who has sowed good seed in his field. His 'enemy comes, and sows tares.' We hear, also, of the consternation excited by the discovery of this fact. To think of such things having found a place in that householder's field! And after all his labour and care! 'Didst not thou sow good seed in thy field? From whence, then, hath it tares?' And yet, in conclusion, notwithstanding all this, and to the still greater surprise of this householder's servants, we hear of this evil, for the present, at least, being allowed to remain. At 'the time of harvest'—but not till then—shall it be taken away.

While the disciples are pondering the meaning of this parable, two others are added, both of them having to do, apparently, with the question of the growth of 'the Kingdom.' Outwardly, it is to develop as 'a grain of mustard seed' does, viz., so as to reach larger dimensions in proportion to its beginning than any other seed known. Inwardly, on the other hand, it is to prevail and conquer in secret, after the manner of 'leaven hid in a lump,' 'until the whole is leavened.'

Thus strictly does Jesus, at this season, observe His new rule. 'Without a parable' He never speaks to 'them' now. This is another of those many points in which the spirit of prophecy, whilst speaking apparently only of others, is found to be describing, perhaps unconsciously, what is pre-eminently true about Him: 'I will open my mouth in parables; I will utter things which have been kept secret from the foundation of the world.'

This, however, is only to 'them,' i.e., to His hearers at large. To His own disciples, after the 'multitude' has been 'sent away,' and when they and He are 'in the house' by themselves, He 'declares the parable of the Tares of the Field.' He explains to them, in so many words, that is to say, who is meant by the 'sower,' viz., Himself; what is meant by the 'field,' viz., the 'world;' who are the 'reapers,' viz., the 'angels;' and what is the appointed time of separation, viz., 'the end of the world.' Also, in regard to those three other parables which immediately follow, viz., those of 'the Treasure hid in the Field,' the 'Pearl of Great Price,' and the 'Net drawn to the Shore,' we find Him observing what amounts, in reality, to a very similar rule. He does not, indeed, exactly 'declare' these parables to His friends; but He appears only to refrain from doing so because He ascertains from themselves that they understand them already. Possibly, this itself is some evidence, on their part, of the success of His plan. The 'little' they began with has been already increased.

They have now become skilful, comparatively speaking, in knowing what parables mean. Perhaps, also, it is for the same reason that He, as it were, finally clenches all these parables, by another parable still. 'Have ye understood all these things? They say unto Him, Yea, Lord. Then said He unto them, Therefore every scribe which is instructed unto the kingdom of heaven is like unto a housholder which bringeth forth out of his treasure things new and old.' This, in brief, is what all these parables ought to be to their minds, viz , so many wellnigh inexhaustible treasures of truth!

When Jesus has 'finished these parables,' He 'departs thence' unto another country, where we hear of them no more. For the present this sample of this peculiar method of instruction has answered its end. It has succeeded in 'adding;' and in 'taking away.' It has instructed the ignorant; and confounded the wise. It has rebuked unbelief; and edified faith. And it has furnished us, therefore, with a striking illustration of the singular wisdom of Christ. No one could have selected an instrument better adapted to the peculiar exigencies of His position. Also, when selected, no one could have employed it with greater judgment and skill. How well this is shewn by the little use made of teaching by 'parables' since! Even in the eyes of the world, the touch of Jesus seems to have consecrated it for ever.

CHAPTER IX

ITS HIGHEST POINT.

Matt. xiv. xv. xvi. 1-20.

ANOTHER of our 'longer stages' now stretches before us. It happens, also, to be a stage of a very diversified kind. Persons and places, some of them never mentioned elsewhere, come before us in turn, mixed up with miracles, parables, explanations, and episodes of various kinds. Yet, amidst it all, with more or less clearness, there is one idea to be traced. Alike in extent and in depth, alike as to unbelief and to faith, there is a steady increase in the impression produced by the Ministry of Christ Jesus.

The opening verses (ch. xiii. 54–58) exemplify this feature very vividly in the way of *taking offence*. Once before we read of His near kinsfolk coming after Him into that part of Galilee in which He was labouring, in order to detach Him from His work. It pleases Him now to leave the rest of Galilee in order to come unto them. The inhabitants of Nazareth are so far from appreciating the attention, that they approve of Him even less than before. They are all 'offended in Him,' it is said. They are 'offended in Him,' notwithstanding the fact that they are compelled, in some respects, to admire Him. 'Whence hath this man this wisdom, and these mighty acts?' With His antecedents, it is a dire offence to them that He should have become what He is. None of His relatives—and there are plenty of them—have done anything of the kind. This is exactly the way of envy, all the world over. The higher its object, the greater its depth. In what follows we see its inevitable punishment, too. 'He did not many mighty works there because of their unbelief.'

The next matter mentioned furnishes a similar illustration in the way of *causing alarm*. Some time before this, Herod the Tetrarch had shut up John the Baptist in prison. After that, he had reluctantly consented to taking his life. Now he hears of another Teacher, and of the mighty works He has done. This is an observable thing of itself. A ruler like Herod would be about the last person in all his dominions to become acquainted with this unobtrusive movement for good. If *he* has heard of Jesus, every one has. All lower heights must have been reached in turn before reaching that summit. The language also employed by Herod, on hearing the report of the doings of Jesus, is a most observable thing. It shews the kind of report he has heard. After hearing it, he is ready to believe even in a rising again from the dead. So far, in fact, as he is concerned, he can only account for it in this way. 'It is John the Baptist; he is risen from the dead; and therefore mighty works do shew forth themselves in him.' From the point of view of Herod's experience, what more could he say?

The course adopted by Jesus of Nazareth on hearing of what Herod had said illustrates the now rapidly growing fame of His ministry, in the way of *observing precaution*. The notice of Herod could be nothing but a hindrance to work such as His. He, therefore, 'withdraws' Himself from it. He withdraws 'by ship'—perhaps as the quickest and least observable way. He withdraws, also, to a 'desert place apart,' as to the least observable spot. Evidently, if the thing be feasible, He desires to be by Himself.

For the present, however, this seems wholly unfeasible, so far as the 'multitudes' are concerned. From all the neighbouring 'cities,' having found out whither He has gone, they follow Him, in amazing numbers, along the shore of the sea.

When He learns this, He 'comes forth' and beholds them; and the sight touches His heart. With all His present desire for retirement, He can only think, for the time, of their wants; and proceeds, therefore, as so often before, to 'heal their sick.' The 'evening' is upon Him—so many are they—by the time He has finished. The disciples, in consequence, urge Him to send the multitudes home. 'This is a desert place, and the time is now past;' tell the people to go away and buy themselves food. 'There is no need of this,' the Master answers; 'do ye give them to eat.' 'How can we give to them,' they reply in effect, 'when we have not enough for ourselves?' 'Bring it to Me, whatever it is.' When they have done so, He bids the multitude sit. Then, in His hands, and with His blessing upon it, it becomes enough for them all. They all 'eat.' They all are 'filled.' Afterwards, when the disciples come, as it were, to clear up, although there were only five small loaves to begin, they fill twelve large baskets with the 'fragments that remain.' They do this, moreover, notwithstanding the fact that no fewer than 'five thousand men' had been at that feast, not counting such women and children as had been able to travel so far.

This novel and striking manifestation of power is followed up in a very significant way. The astonished disciples are forthwith 'constrained' to re-enter the ship that had brought them, and to start across the sea by themselves. The still lingering multitudes, when these are gone, are made to go too. Jesus is at last by Himself.

At the same time, in another sense, He is not by Himself. He is holding communion with God 'in prayer.' And He is doing so with such earnestness that we do not hear of Him again for some hours. The 'evening' had closed in at the time He began. The 'fourth watch' has arrived, the dawn is approaching, before the disciples see Him again.

Was this special earnestness connected with the growing exigencies of His work at that time?

When the disciples do see Him again, it is in most marvellous guise. They are vainly struggling, in the midst of the sea, against contrary winds. They become aware of a Form approaching them over the tempestuous waves. Supposing it, at first, to be a 'spirit,' they cry out in alarm. Finding it, by and by, instead of this, to be their Master Himself, they are correspondingly re-assured. So much so, indeed, that one among them is immediately ready for a most perilous step. 'Lord,' he says, 'if it be Thou, let me come unto Thee on the water.' See the point to which the faith of this Peter has now come about Christ. The subsequent failure of his confidence as he endeavours to walk on the water, his consequent appeal for help to his Master, and the effectual help immediately rendered to him, are graciously overruled to raise that faith to a still higher degree. 'O thou of little faith, wherefore didst thou doubt?' To that question they all feel now that they have nothing to say. They have no reason now for doubting Jesus, let Him say what He may. In sudden silence, therefore—for the 'wind has ceased'—they acknowledge as much. Both by action and word they openly confess Him to be 'Son of God beyond doubt!'

This striking confession may prepare us for another, of which we shall presently hear. Meanwhile, in quite another locality, we see the confidence of men in His power. He disembarks in the 'land of Gennesaret.' As soon as the inhabitants discover who has arrived, the whole country-side is alive. All the sick from all round about are hastily brought to His feet. There is but one thing they desire—to touch the hem of His garment. There is but one result when they do—they are made perfectly whole.

After this—for the first time in this account of the ministry of Jesus—the city of Jerusalem is mentioned. Even in that proud ecclesiastical metropolis, the fame of this provincial teacher seems to be at last making a stir. At any rate, some of the 'Scribes and Pharisees' who belong to it have 'come down to Jesus,' and are now observing His work. The reception they meet with must have greatly augmented that stir. Anything more revolutionary and uncompromising, from their point of view, than the answer of Jesus could not well be conceived. When they take His disciples to task for the measure of liberty which He has allowed them, they are taken to task in their turn. The very words also of their own prophetical scriptures are deliberately quoted against them. And even those multitudes who had been so long accustomed to receive their teaching without misgiving or question are 'called' up, and taught to regard it as something radically unsound. Such war to the knife appears to have astonished the disciples themselves; and must have greatly deepened the impression made as well on others as on them.

It is not surprising therefore to read, next, of Jesus 'withdrawing' again. This time He does so to a part of the country where we have never heard of Him yet, viz., where the territory of Israel meets with that of Sidon and Tyre. Yet even there He is known. One is there, at any rate, who knows as much of Him as any in Galilee do. She knows His power. She knows His mercy. She knows and believes in His claims. 'Have mercy on me, O Lord, Thou Son of David; my daughter is grievously vexed with a devil.' What a lesson to those 'disciples' who hear her cry out! Also, what a revelation to *them*, to find *her* ultimately commended and blessed!

Once more the Saviour is near His favourite lake. Again the thronging multitudes are bringing their afflicted ones to His feet. Again those afflicted ones, however afflicted, are relieved by His power. This time, the effect on the bystanders seems to be greater than ever before. The multitude 'wonder' when they see what takes place. Much as they had seen previously, they seem to be seeing more now; even 'the dumb to speak, the maimed to be whole, the lame to walk, and the blind to see.' And, as they see it, they are unable to refrain from giving glory to God. A loud murmur of devout praise rises up from them all.

This special feeling of wonder seems to have led for a time to some degree of forgetfulness even of hunger and thirst. So, at least, the words of Jesus Himself seem to imply: 'They continue with Me now three days, and have nothing to eat.' In other respects the general circumstances are almost identical with some related to us before. What wonder, therefore, that we find this 'history' repeating itself, as it were; and that, hearing again, as we do, of so many in want, we also hear again of the same tenderness and discrimination of compassion, the same manifested shortness of supply, the same inadequacy of resource on the part of the disciples, the same weakness of faith, the same fulness of blessing, the same bountifulness of relief! To say nothing, in addition, of the same careful absence of waste, the same ample abundance of evidence, the same exact computation of numbers, and the same anxiety, when all is completed, to send the multitude home!

Unbelief, however, is not to be silenced even by accumulation of proof. The Pharisees and Sadducees, therefore—united for once—demand additional 'signs.' Inasmuch, however, as additional signs upon earth can hardly be thought of, even by them, they ask to have them 'from heaven.' Jesus, in answer to this, with one brief and well-merited word of reproof, and one also of mysterious promise, exposes them and departs.

He has crossed the sea and reached the 'other side,' but is still full of this subject. So much so that He earnestly enjoins on His own disciples to 'beware' of that settled and deadly 'leaven,' of which they had just seen an example. It is not, however, until He has explained Himself further that they comprehend what He means. Then they appear to lay it to heart with a will. Not only do they understand that they are to listen to Him, they also understand that to their former teachers they are to listen no more.

From such a conclusion it is but a step to one very much wider. Once again we find Jesus of Nazareth on the outskirts of the land. This time He is in 'the parts of Cæsarea Philippi,' under the shadow of Mount Hermon, and far away to the north. His disciples are with Him alone. He takes the opportunity of ascertaining the results of His labours, so far. In His judgment, the time has come for this step. He asks them first, therefore, as we should say, about the public at large. 'Whom do men say that I am?' The answers given vary in form, but are one in effect. ' They speak of Thee as being as great as any one ever hitherto sent.' 'He saith unto them, But whom say ye that I am?' The most forward amongst them answers for all. 'Thou art the Christ, the Son of the Living God.'

The mountain solitudes which hear that confession do not understand its importance.

Its exceeding importance in the eyes of Him who received it is made in many ways plain.

First of all, by the extraordinary fervour which marks His reply: '*Blessed* art thou' (whoever thou art) who hast outspoken those words.

Next, by the emphatic directness of its application and address. 'Blessed art *thou, Simon Bar-jona*,' who hast spoken out thus. Others there are who think as much, and who are therefore 'blessed' as well. But not so blessed as thou.

Also, by the height of origin to which this confession is traced. 'Flesh and blood hath not revealed it unto thee, but My Father which is in heaven.'

Also, yet, by the decided progress of which it is pronounced to be proof. 'I say unto thee, that thou art *Peter*.' I pronounce thee to be a 'stone' indeed —in fact, the first stone in My Church.

Finally, by the future hopes of which it is hailed as a pledge. Having thus actually begun, He can also go on, to build. Also, He can build in safety now, because on the 'rock' of this truth. None of His enemies, not even 'the gates of hell,' shall be able to overthrow what He builds. Neither shall any of His friends, though in themselves the weakest, be unable to assist in His work. Every one of them, rather, thus confessing Him, shall be, in fact, as Himself. 'I will give unto thee the keys of the kingdom of heaven: and whatsoever thou shalt bind on earth shall be bound in heaven: and whatsoever thou shalt loose on earth shall be loosed in heaven.'

Thus solemnly is this first open confession of Jesus of Nazareth as the Christ, welcomed by Him as the culmination of His strictly ministerial work.

For the present, however, in regard to it, He enjoins silence upon all. Indirectly, they have all joined with Peter in acknowledging Him as the Christ. They must be content with that for the present. Much has to happen before they can be commissioned to proclaim Him to the world.

PART IV.

THE PASSION OF CHRIST.

CHAPTER I.

A CHANGE OF VOICE.

Matt. xvi. 21-28, xvii. xviii. xix. xx.

The moment a traveller has left any station of importance fairly behind him, he begins to think of the next. It was so with the illustrious Traveller of the story before us. No sooner has He been openly acknowledged and saluted as Christ, than He begins to think of His death. That death, as it were, is now waiting for Him in the path He is treading. In following that path, it is the great thing for which He has next to prepare. Knowing this, He naturally begins to think of it, and also to speak of it, much. He would have His disciples begin to prepare for it too. He begins to 'shew' unto them, therefore (as we noticed before), how He 'must go unto Jerusalem, and suffer many things of the chief priests and scribes, and be killed, and be raised again the third day.' He continues, also, so we are told, to speak in this manner 'from that time forth.' Henceforward, there is something of the shadow of death in almost all that He says.

How great a change this implied on His part, is shewn by the change to which it leads on the part of

His disciples. On Peter, especially, the result is most marked. Only just before he had saluted his Master as the greatest of men. if not as very much more. 'Thou art the Christ, the Son of the living God.' Now he dares to find open fault with Him for what He is saying. Now, by his gestures, he even seems inclined to hold Him back from such speech. He 'takes Him,' it is said, and begins to 'rebuke' Him. 'What can the Master be thinking of to be thus hard on Himself? Why is He predicting what cannot possibly become true about Him?'

If this ardent disciple had not been startled out of himself by what he had heard, he could never have forgot himself thus.

The reception which his 'rebuke' meets with, is of a most remarkable kind. In a different way, Jesus attaches as much importance to it as to his previous confession. He had traced that to heaven. He traces this to hell. He repels it, therefore, with a degree of fervour only equalled by that with which He had welcomed the other. He even addresses Peter, in consequence, as once before He had addressed the Adversary himself. That Evil One, in the wilderness, had tempted Him by the offer of a magnificent crown. He refused it at once. Peter's present language amounts to a suggestion that He should spare Himself an equally terrible cross. He refuses this in like manner. Come from whom it may, the suggestion is as hateful to Him as was the direct offer of Satan. And

Peter himself, therefore, who has made the suggestion, is addressed as a like 'Adversary' for so doing. 'Get thee behind Me, Satan: thou art an offence unto Me: thy thoughts are man's thoughts, not God's.'

This to the man to whom He had said, only a little before, 'God has taught thee this, and not man!'

The distance between these two utterances is the measure of the lesson which the disciples have to be taught.

Their Master, therefore, next presents it to them from a different side. In language, the force of which they would better appreciate by and by, He teaches them that *they* must suffer as well as Himself. 'Any man' whatever, in short, wishing to 'come after' Him, must be prepared to 'deny himself' in like manner. 'Bearing the cross' was their duty as well as His. It was also their wisdom. It was their only wisdom, in fact. After the 'sufferings' would follow the 'glory' of Christ. The utmost endured for His sake would be more than made up in that glory. So much so, indeed, that the only true way of really 'finding' their lives was by 'losing' them in that manner.

He adds, that an opportunity of witnessing something of this glory (and so, of testing the value and truth of these declarations) would be furnished to some of them before they 'tasted of death.'

The fulfilment of this promise came to pass about a week from that date. Peter, James, and John are taken up into 'a high mountain apart.' For the time, they are almost in a separate world. Their Master's appearance is 'transfigured' with glory so as they had never seen it before. Certain chief representatives of the inspiration and piety of the past are seen with Him also. Full of rapture, all that Peter desires is to stay for evermore in that scene. Presently, in an overshadowing cloud of brightness, they hear a mysterious 'voice' which proclaims, 'This is My beloved Son, in whom I am well pleased; hear ye Him.' Then the vision is gone; the mountain is bare; they are again with 'Jesus alone.'

Again for the present, they are to tell no man of the vision they have seen. Not, in fact, till the 'Son of Man be risen from the dead' are they to speak of its secrets. This dark announcement was followed by many surmisings, and by much instruction respecting the expected return of Elias, and the mission of John the Baptist, and his rejection and death. And this, in turn, led to another explicit mention of the coming passion of Christ. 'Likewise also shall the Son of Man suffer' at the hands of mankind.

The sufferings of Christ, however, are to complete His work, not to impede it. Jesus seems to be mindful of this when He comes down from the mount. During His absence, those disciples whom He had left behind had been trying their hands in vain on a peculiarly distressing and difficult case of demoniac possession. Seeing Him return, the all-but despairing father of the suffering little one comes and implores His help. Immediately—notwithstanding the fact that the thought of His own sufferings is still present to His mind; as also, it seems, is the cause of them in the unbelief of the age, together with the near proximity of them in the appointed order of time—Jesus terminates those of the child. 'O faithless and perverse generation, how long shall I be with you? How long shall I bear with you? Bring him hither to Me.' The child is brought; the devil rebuked; the deliverance wrought. A lasting lesson to the perplexed disciples on the omnipotence of true faith.

After this we find Jesus and His disciples 'abiding' again—or, as some have it, 'gathering together' again —in the familiar regions of Galilee. We also find the same general characteristics, whilst they are staying there, in the tone of His words.

As before, for example, we find Him speaking of His approaching death with a degree of explicitness which causes the disciples—though they shew it now in a different manner—to be 'exceedingly grieved.' The chief difference now seems to be in the express mention of that cruel betrayal which was to lead to His death. 'The Son of Man shall be delivered into the hands of men.' As they come gradually nearer to the place of His suffering, He gradually reveals more to them of that fast-gathering storm.

As before, also, we find Him directing His chief instructions now to that little band of disciples from whom He is to be separated so soon. The miracle of the Transfiguration had been for the instruction of Peter, James, and John. The miracle of the coin in the fish's mouth seems to be for that of Peter alone. Afterwards, the lesson taught by it as to the paramount necessity of avoiding all unnecessary offence, is enforced further by calling a little child, and setting him in the midst, and making use of him as a kind of living text on this subject. And, after that again, the question of Peter as to the proper limit of forgiveness in the case of an offending brother is utilized in a similar manner. Also, in all the instruction thus offered to the disciples on these various points, we seem to note a special appropriateness to their circumstances at this time. Only a little before, by means of the confession of Peter, Christ had founded His Church. In a little time after (as He was perpetually reminding them), He was to be taken away from that Church. Now, therefore, is the time to remind them again of its existence and rights. Now, also, is the time to warn them of the certain rise of offences within it; and to enlighten them also respecting the wisest methods of dealing therewith. The Church thus founded must be listened to on pain of separation therefrom. It is a grievous thing to cause just offence even to the weakest of its members. It is infinitely more grievous, by not forgiving such offences, to offend against God. Worthy lessons these, and weighty ones too, for all times of the Church. Doubly opportune for its infant condition, and when just about to be left.

'When Jesus has finished these sayings, He departs from Galilee, and comes into the borders of Judæa beyond Jordan.'

While staying there also, it is to His disciples still that His chief instructions are given.

The ailing multitudes come, it is true, and are healed. The Pharisees, also, with their insidious questions respecting marriage and divorce, come to Him, and are answered. But the answer received by them, if not intended, in the first instance, for the special enlightenment of the disciples, is exactly of such a nature as first to revolutionise, and then to establish, their ideas on these points. This is shewn by the fact that the closing inquiry on these subjects is addressed to their Master, not by the Pharisees, but by them.

In a similar way, the 'little children' that are then brought to Christ for His blessing, are employed by Him to teach certain lessons to the 'disciples' respecting His kingdom and those who really belong to it, which they appear to have needed specially at that particular time.

In a similar way, again, the case of the young man who believed himself to have 'lack' of nothing, either for this world or the next, is employed by the Saviour to teach the 'disciples' how hard it is for those who have 'great earthly possessions,' to secure heavenly treasures as well. It is the same 'disciples,' once more, who are encouraged, on the other hand, to hope for all in the future, because of their having left all for Christ's sake. And it is these same 'disciples,' in the last place, who are solemnly warned, by means of the parable of the Labourers in the Vineyard, that God does not ultimately decide in these matters according to the principles or expectations of men. 'The first shall be last, and the last first.' So the parable is headed. So it is also wound up. Nothing is there which it is more important for the 'disciples' of Christ to remember. Nothing is there, at the same time, which they are more apt to forget.

At last the Jordan is left behind, and Jesus is 'going up' to Jerusalem. How special still His instructions! 'He takes the twelve disciples apart.' How express also His announcement, not of the fact only, but of the precise manner now, of His death. 'They shall deliver Him unto the Gentiles to mock, and to scourge, and to crucify.' Coming nearer still, He reveals more still of that fast-gathering storm.

This principle is exemplified next in yet one other way. The mother of the two sons of Zebedee comes to Him with a special request, which is a mark at once of her ignorance and her faith. 'Command that these my two sons may sit, one on Thy right hand, and one on Thy left hand, in Thy kingdom.' Both this unwise request, and the indignation it arouses, Jesus turns at once to good use. None are truly great in His kingdom, unless they resemble Himself. None resemble Him less than those who are looked upon as the great ones of the earth. *His* one desire is to supply that ministry which it is *their* great desire to receive. That very death of His, in fact, to which He is travelling, is the crowning proof of this truth. Besides being all that He had told them before—besides being the result of deadly hatred and treachery—besides being the occasion of indescribable torture and shame—it was also a long-designed and voluntary surrender of life itself, on His part, for other men's good. Herein lies the heart of the whole. To be 'a ransom for many!' That is the feature in it, when coming closest to it, which is found eclipsing the rest.

A gracious miracle winds up this part of the story. As Jesus passes out of Jericho, and begins the ascent which is to conduct Him to the city of His crucifixion, two blind men who are sitting together by the wayside find out who it is, and cry out. The multitudes hear them, and bid them be silent. Jesus hears them, and bids them approach. They do so, and prefer their request. 'Moved with compassion,' He touches their eyes. 'Straightway' they are able to see, and begin to follow His steps. It is a sight which seems to have impressed the Evangelist much. It should do the same with ourselves. The shadow of death is in front of Jesus as He goes up to Jerusalem; the light of mercy behind!

CHAPTER II.

A CHANGE OF ATTITUDE.

Matt. xxi. xxii. 1–14.

JERUSALEM itself is at last in sight. Jesus has reached the Mount of Olives, on the eastern side of the city. How does He prepare to go in?

In a manner wholly different from anything recorded of Him before. Two of the disciples are sent to fetch an ass and her colt, of which He has told them, from a neighbouring village. In case of any difficulty in obtaining possession of these animals, those who go for them are to inform the owners that they are 'needed' by 'the Lord.' To the authority implied in that statement there will not be any demur.

According to the Evangelist, the peculiar significance of this proceeding lies in its relation to a certain prophecy spoken some few hundred years previously. At the time of its utterance, the city of Jerusalem was part of the great empire of Persia, and so under alien rule. What this prophecy promised to 'the daughter of Zion' is the privilege of 'beholding' a 'king' of her own; a king, also, who shall 'come' to her, as it were, in a way of his own, viz., 'riding' in 'meekness' upon just such animals as those for which Jesus had sent.

By sending for them now, therefore, and entering Jerusalem upon them, He practically identifies Himself with the prophecy in question. Also in spirit He does the same, by 'requisitioning' (as we have seen) the assistance He needs, after the manner of kings. And the same, again, by allowing the disciples to caparison the ass and her colt in such manner as their circumstances allowed; and by permitting the multitude at large to strew the ground with garments and branches, and bless Him aloud as the 'Son of David,' 'coming in the name of the Lord.'

Altogether, this manner of entry shows plainly enough what He means. It is a spectacle signifying to the people of Jerusalem just so much, and no more. He thereby asserts His rights, but not His majesty yet. He appears before them as their native-born, long-foretold King, but not at present in order to do the work of a king—at any rate, not that part of the work of a king which consists in punishing the wrong-doers. It is rather, in fact, as a royal 'visitor,' than as a commissioned 'judge,' that He comes:—like the figure of Justice (shall we say?), with her sword sheathed, but still retaining her scales.

Something of this appears to be recognised by the multitudes present. Whilst they are thus proclaiming Him King with loud praises to God, the whole city to which they are approaching is agitated thereby, and cries out to know who it is that approaches them thus. The multitudes answer and say, 'This is Jesus, the Prophet of Nazareth in Galilee.' Whether or not they fully know it, both answers are right. Both, in fact, are required. He is at once a King and a Prophet; at once lowly and high; the Royal Son of David, yet Jesus of Nazareth still; supreme in dignity, and in meekness as well.

The action of the Saviour when He finally reaches the city carries on the same thoughts. The first thing He does there is to 'enter the temple of God, and cast out all them that sold and bought in the temple, and overthrow the tables of the money-changers, and the seats of them that sold doves,' saying unto them, as He does so, 'It is written, My house shall be called a house of prayer, but ye have made it a den of thieves.' In other words, He exercises in the temple of God what are known as 'visitatorial powers,' and treats it just as any other legitimate king would treat any house of his own. Further than this, however, at this juncture, He does not proceed. On the contrary, instead of now inflicting on such evil-doers the punishment they deserve, we find Him engaged in the merciful work of 'healing' the 'blind and the lame,' whose misery has taught them to find Him out and come to Him there.

Even when the chief priests and scribes, the persons most responsible for the evil denounced by Him, seeing the wonderful things which He does, and hearing the very children in consequence repeating some of the salutations with which He had been greeted on His way to the city, are indignant with Him for not at once suppressing such significant greetings, He still pursues the same line. After defending the children, and rebuking His foes, He contents Himself with departing from them, and seeking quiet elsewhere.

On His return the next morning, an incident happens which serves to shew how much He could have done at that time in the way of punishment, had such been His design. A little way off the road that led to Jerusalem from Bethany (the place to which He had retired on the previous evening), He beholds a fig-tree giving every promise of abundance of fruit. On coming up, however, He finds sufficient evidence that this mere promise is all. There is 'nothing' on it but 'leaves.' Immediately, as in a kind of acted parable, the tree is sentenced to destruction. Immediately, also, the sentence is carried into effect. The tree 'withers away.' Then the astonished disciples are assured that, with sufficient faith, they could do greater things still; even to the extent of removing the solid mountain itself on which they were standing, if such a thing were required, and casting it into the sea. How easily therefore, as well as how justly, could the 'barren fig-tree' of Jerusalem be destroyed by their Master! There is everything in the condition of that city to provoke such a doom. There is nothing to prevent it, except the limits which He has placed on Himself.

These same limits will not now be overstepped by Him, happen what may; not even the most violent collision with the ringleaders of evil. Now that He has come again into the temple of God, He sees the chief priests and elders of the people approaching Him in a body. The question which they submit is one which implies the fullest perception, and yet the flattest denial, of the royal rights He has claimed. 'By what authority doest Thou these things? and who gave Thee this authority?' The moderation of His answer is as observable as its wisdom. By a simple reference to the mission of John the Baptist, who had so plainly testified to Himself, He at once justifies His own language and silences theirs. But there He stops short. He effectually defends His authority. He does not attempt to avenge it. Neither does He do so really, in that striking succession of parables by which He supplements His reply. In the parable of the Two Sons in the Vineyard, for example, there is much faithful rebuke. These men, like the barren fig-tree inspected just before, promised much without yielding anything. They are, therefore, shewn those despised 'publicans and harlots,' who at first refused to obey, but afterwards 'repented and went,' going into the kingdom of God 'before' them. In the parable of the Householder and his Vineyard, again, with its incisive application from the Old Testament Scriptures, besides similar faithful rebuke, there is solemn warning of judgment to come. And in the subsequent parable of the Marriage Feast which the King made for his Son, similar rebuke and similar warning are both intensified by its peculiarly solemn and individualising conclusion. It is not only of a body of men, but of one man by himself, that this parable speaks in the end. 'Bind *him* hand and foot; and cast *him* into "that" outer darkness,' where, though there is nothing seen, there is so much heard, telling of unavailing remorse. In all this, however, all the evil spoken of is either future or past. Outside the parables themselves, the men addressed by them are touched in conscience alone. 'They perceive' that the speaker, in these parables, has *spoken* of them. But they are so far from being made to *suffer* by Him, that they are planning instead how to cause Him to suffer by them. The right is His. He leaves the power with them. He is no less distinct in claiming the one, than in *not* exerting the other, as yet.

Was ever any one more faithful in speech and more gentle in deed? Could there be at once a truer, and yet a lowlier, King?

CHAPTER III.

A WIDE CONSPIRACY.

Matt. xxii. 15-46.

THE direct attacks of the Jewish rulers on the position and authority now claimed by Jesus of Nazareth having only succeeded in shaking their own, they next betake themselves to indirect modes of assault.

The Pharisees are the first to try their hands in this line. How ready this Man is in instructing, how prompt in replying, how faithful in rebuking, they have seen for themselves. They will turn these qualities to His ruin. They will 'entangle Him in His talk.'

It is in connection with the claims so much resented by them that they make this attempt. There were two opposite powers at that time in existence, both feared by them much; the power of Cæsar, and that of the multitude. They will endeavour to embroil this 'King of the Jews' with one of these two.

On every ground the plan adopted by them appears sure of success. In the first place, they mean to test Him by a question which is of an exceedingly difficult kind. 'Tell us, what thinkest Thou? Is it lawful to give tribute unto Cæsar, or not?' In the next place, those are to put this question to Him, some of whom will be ready at once to turn His answer to evil, on whichever side it may be. If the 'disciples of the Pharisees' among them do not denounce Him in consequence, the 'Herodians' will. If the Herodians do not, the Pharisees will. In the last place, the question itself is to be so introduced as to divert His mind from any suspicion of evil, and so, from any endeavour to protect Himself in any way from their wiles. 'Master, we know that Thou art true, and teachest the way of God in truth, and carest not for any one: for Thou regardest not the person of men.' How is He to escape from so subtle a snare?

As a matter of fact, He does so by the simplest possible means. First, the flattery is rebuked. 'Why tempt ye Me, ye hypocrites?' Then the fallacy is exposed. 'Shew Me the tribute money.' They hand Him in reply a Roman denarius or 'penny,' having on it the usual 'image and superscription of Cæsar.' What does their acceptance and use of this coin amount to in effect? What but a confession that God has allowed them, for the time, to be under Cæsar's yoke? In that twofold fact lies the twofold answer to the question they ask. Render to Cæsar those things which God has given to him for the time. Render to God those other things which He has reserved to Himself.

The messengers hear, and marvel, and go away, discomfited men.

After the Pharisees and Herodians have been disposed of, the Sadducees appear on the scene. These disbelievers in the possibility of a rising again from the dead come to Him 'the same day' with a question founded on the current belief in that doctrine. In the case of a man dying without issue, the Law of Moses enjoined on his surviving brother to take his widow to wife. In this way it had once come to pass—according to them—that no fewer than seven brothers in one family had all had the same woman to wife. Supposing them all to rise again from the dead, whose wife, of all the seven, ought this woman to be? What has Jesus to say, as a teacher of truth—what has He to say, as a ruler and judge—in regard to this point?

It is a skilful question—they suppose an unanswerable one—with the object in view.

Yet how easy, again, when once given, is His solution thereof!

'In the resurrection they neither marry, nor are given in marriage, but are as the angels of God in heaven.'

With that simple yet profound announcement, the whole substratum of the difficulty, and, therefore, of course the whole superstructure as well, are taken away.

Add to which, it is easy to shew that this very doctrine of the resurrection from the dead was taught them in reality by one of the names which it had pleased God to give to Himself in the most ancient portion of their canonical books. 'The God of Abraham' never meant the God of one who had ceased to exist.

The multitude are 'astonished,' the Sadducees 'silenced,' by these sudden flashes of truth.

Once more the Pharisees, but this time without the Herodians, endeavour to bring about His disgrace. They appear to be stimulated to this fresh effort by hearing that their rivals have failed. How sweet the thought of at once confounding Him and distancing them! Anyway, they now approach Him from a different side. One of their number, a known expert in the study of the National Law, stands forward as a kind of champion to 'tempt' Him by its means. Of all the commandments proclaimed in the Book of the Law, which did He look upon as the greatest? which should first be obeyed? It was a difficult question, no doubt; a perilous labyrinth, out of which it was by no means easy for any reputation to escape, as it were, with its life. Yet, even here, such a 'Master' as this cleanser of the temple ought to be able to see His way through.

How fully He does so is soon and easily shewn. The most important of all the commandments is that which lies at the basis of all. The first thing required of all creatures is to love their Creator. They cannot do this too much. The better they observe this first and great commandment, the better also they will observe that which comes next. The more they love God, the more truly they will love their neighbours as well. Moreover, if they do these two things, they do all. Beyond these 'two commandments' nothing is insisted on in the way of duty, either by the inspiration of Moses himself, or by all that has followed him since.

A sudden revolution is the immediate consequence of this final repulse. Hitherto, various conspirators have put questions to Christ. Now the case is reversed; He puts a question to them. Before the discomfited Pharisees have dispersed, while they still remain 'gathered together,' He follows up their defeat. Practically and secretly, if not in so many words, they have been disputing His claim to be Christ. How far, as a matter of fact, do they understand that question themselves? What do they really know about Christ? 'We know that He is to be the Son of David,' they might probably say. How then do they understand that which David says about Him in spirit?

> 'The Lord said unto my Lord,
> Sit Thou on my right hand,
> Till I put Thine enemies underneath Thy feet.'

Here we have David, in so many words, speaking of Christ as his 'Lord.' How can He be, at the same time, his descendant or 'Son?'

This deeply significant inquiry completely baffles them all. 'No man is able to answer Him a word.' It does very much more. Taken in conjunction with their previous disasters, it puts a complete end to all word-attacks on His position and claims. 'From that day forth no man dares ask Him any more questions.' In this kind of battle He has gained the victory along the whole line. Not only now has He asserted His kingship; He has proved it as well.

CHAPTER IV.

A FINAL WARNING.

Matt. xxiii.

IN the temporary silence which follows that overthrow of His enemies which we described in our last, how does Jesus behave Himself towards them? In what language does He speak concerning them to those that stand by?

In such language as to put especial honour both on their office and work. 'The Scribes and Pharisees sit in Moses' seat.' Their duty is to explain and enforce that which Moses has taught. To obey them, therefore, when they do this faithfully, is to obey Moses himself. It is also, He implies, and that with much emphasis, to do what is pleasing to Him. '*Whatsoever* they bid you' in this manner, that 'do and observe' (R.V.).

These are striking words in themselves. Long before now He had made the announcement, 'I am not come to destroy the Law, but to fulfil it.' Here He upholds the authority of those undertaking to explain it. Some time before He had Himself shewn respect to this kind of authority, when directing Peter to pay for both of them the Temple-tribute at Capernaum. Now, on all who listen to Him He lays the injunction that they should shew the same deference too.

Still more striking, when regarded in its circumstances, will this language be found. What a juncture is that chosen by Him for this declaration of His will! Just after the men referred to have been conspiring in the most unscrupulous manner against His authority, He is thus scrupulous about theirs. Just when they have most disgraced their office, He honours it most. In the time of their hope He had withstood them. In this time of their despondency He upholds them. What generous forbearance, what considerate pity, what meekness still, we have here!

What sedulous faithfulness also! It is important for the 'multitudes,' and more so for His 'disciples,' that they should honour every one to whom honour is due. It is still more important for all, that they should not be seduced thereby into the commission of sin. Hence the cautions which follow. Honour the injunctions of these teachers, but not their example. Their practice is indifferent, even when their precepts are right. On the one hand, 'they say, and do not.' The more onerous and irksome the requirements of Moses, the greater their eagerness in laying these requirements, not on themselves, but on others. On the other hand, in all such outward obedience as they themselves render to Moses, there is an unworthy motive at work. To appear pious before men in their dress and demeanour, and to receive honour from men whenever appearing before them in public, are the real aims they pursue. Whereas, with you, My servants, these are the very things which you must most diligently avoid. Pride, in short, is their object; but humility must be yours. And most wisely so, too. For no one shall ever be truly 'exalted,' but he that 'humbles' himself.

After the misled, the misleaders—after the too confiding followers, the faithless guides—are admonished. And that, of course, as with greater cause, so with more manifest force. Wilful deceivers as such 'hypocrites' are; first of themselves, and then of others; what is to come to them except 'woe?' Most sternly in appearance, therefore, yet most mercifully in reality, is their 'refuge of lies' assailed by this truth. Some seven times over its ominous thunders are made to sound in their ears. Even yet shall they know, if the thing be possible, both their danger and sin!

How much, for example, both of danger and sin, is to be seen in the effect of their conduct on the very gateway of life! Instead of shewing the way in (as they ought to have done) to the rest of the world, they are closing it fast against all—against others, against themselves!

How much, again, there is, both of danger and sin, even where they seem to succeed! Wonderfully great, in the way of proselyting, are the efforts they make. Wonderfully insignificant are the results attained—except in accomplishing ruin.

After all, however, with their teaching, is this a thing of surprise? How should these be able to guide men into fulness of light, who only half see it themselves? And how can such unhappy imperfection of vision be more convincingly evidenced than by the exaggerated views entertained by these teachers, of the mere corners of truth? To see the ornaments of the Temple, but not the Temple on which their real beauty depends; to see the gifts on the altar, but not the altar which makes them acceptable; to see the throne of God, but not to discern the sovereignty of Him that sitteth thereon—is to see far more error than truth. This more-than-half-blindness which thinks it sees, is worse than total blindness itself.

The same thing is true of those petty and partial observances which pretend to be all. No rebellion is more offensive than that false scrupulousness which 'strains out the gnat and swallows the camel.'

Nor is any defilement worse than that false reformation which, by dealing with the outside alone, prevents the true cleansing of all.

Nor is any deformity worse than that mere beauty of surface which conceals all foulness within.

Nor is any profaneness worse than that spurious reverence which does not honour the servants of God until they are out of the way. This empty worship of names is nothing else, in fact, than another form of that same hatred of reality which, in old days, persecuted the prophets themselves.

Awful, therefore, is the shadow cast thereby on 'this generation.' The true inheritor of the spirit of the past, it is also the heir of its guilt. Of all overt sin known, nothing is like this persecution of God's representatives in proving enmity of heart against Him. In regard to nothing, consequently, is He wont to exact a stricter account. Never yet, also, had any generation surpassed this one—as would only too soon and too fully be proved—in such display of this hate. Upon it, therefore, is to descend the punishment, in all its fulness, that has been held back for so long. This is the rule with the long-suffering judgment of God. The generation which finally 'fills the cup' up has to exhaust it as well.

As this Meekest of Kings foresees these terrible griefs and foretells them, a sorrow of almost equal intensity seizes Himself. Often and often, in bygone years, with tenderest love,—what a glimpse this gives us into the mysterious depths both of His nature and heart!—would He have gathered together the 'children' of Jerusalem in safety and peace. Just as often, with invincible aversion, had His offers of love been rejected! Never, now, will He make them again! When next He comes, that 'House' of theirs will have gone; and another spirit, if not another race, shall have risen up in their stead!

CHAPTER V.

A FINAL PREDICTION.

Matt. xxiv. xxv.

AFTER Jesus had taken His solemn farewell of the Temple, He appears to have once more made His way towards the Mount of Olives and Bethany. Some of the disciples look back on the buildings which they are leaving behind, and admire their beauty and strength. Then, 'coming up,' they 'point them out' to the attention of Christ. Only see what buildings are here!

Great as ye see them to be—so He replies in effect—the time is coming when, as buildings, they shall cease to exist. 'Verily, I say unto you, There shall not be left here one stone upon another, that shall not be thrown down.'

To this strange announcement, as it certainly sounded to them, the disciples have nothing to say—except among themselves—for a time. Not till the Mount of Olives is reached, not till their Master has taken His seat on it and they find themselves with Him alone, do they venture to question Him about it. Then they have much to inquire. They would know the time, they would know the manner, they would know the full purport, of the ominous things of which He has just spoken to the Pharisees and themselves. 'Tell us, when shall these things be?' and what shall be the sign of Thy coming, and of the end of the world?

His answer opens, where their questions left off, with the key and crux of the whole. On no point will there be so much necessity for 'taking heed' of mistake, as in regard to the nature and time of 'the end.' They must learn this, to begin. Many observers will be so wholly mistaken, as to suppose that to be the 'end,' which will prove, instead, to be merely the 'beginning of sorrows.' Many professed disciples, again, will be so offended and deceived and alienated by outward persecutions, and by inward treasons and heresies and corruptions, as to fail of 'enduring to the end;'—and so will prove themselves to be, in fact, no disciples at all. For all this, however, the good news of the kingdom will gradually spread over the face of the world until all the nations, in all parts, shall have heard its 'witness' themselves. By that time this present 'age' will be almost touching its 'end.' When every nation has had its opportunity, the day of opportunity will be close upon setting. The 'day' that is to follow will be of a different kind!

Before that time, however, there is to come another 'end'—as it were, predictive of this. This earlier visitation will be distinguished, first, by its comparative narrowness. It is only to affect the race identified with the land of 'Judæa.' By its singular rapidity, next. Its special 'sign' is to be the appearance in Judæa of that 'abomination of desolation which was spoken of by Daniel the prophet.' The moment that 'sign' is perceived, let all those who 'understand' it seek to escape for their lives. By its unexampled severity, in the third place. That 'elect' race itself would never survive 'those days' unless their duration were 'shortened.' By its clear significance, in the fourth place. Notwithstanding many false pretensions and some real perplexities, it will be an unmistakeable manifestation or 'presence' of Christ. Not in the 'wilderness,' for example, where none would see it; nor yet in the 'secret chambers,' where none could find it ; but, like the lightning itself, in heaven above, where none can miss it—will *this* 'parousia' be. By its unavoidable certainty, in the last place. Spiritually speaking, the 'race' referred to, at the time referred to, will be but a body of death. Where else, therefore, except 'gathered' around it, can the birds of death be ?

When the 'tribulation of those days' shall have at last come to its close, the signs of that other and later one, which has been spoken of before, shall 'immediately' begin to appear. They will be such as shall harmonise exactly and strikingly with its wider scope and ulterior date. Such perturbations and changes shall take place, for example, amongst the lights of heaven, as cannot fail to change the look, and affect the well-being, of everything upon earth. To these there will succeed, in turn, causing bitter sorrow to 'all the tribes of the earth,' a greater thing still, even '*the* sign' (whatever its exact character) 'of the Son of Man in heaven.' To this, naturally, nothing less than the actual 'presence' of the 'Son of Man Himself coming in the clouds of heaven with power and great glory.' And to that (again naturally in connection with such a manifestation), the solemn sending forth of 'the "angels" of the Son of Man, with a great sound of a trumpet,' for the purpose of gathering together from all parts of the universe all those that are His.

These are mighty changes, beyond any doubt. But let none imagine them, on that account, to be matters of doubt. On the contrary, they are as certain, at their appointed period, as are the yearly seasons themselves. 'The fig-tree,' on this point, has 'her parable' for our learning. Her opening buds are so many tokens that the warm breath of the coming summer has been already felt by her life. Just so of the secret forces by which the changes spoken of are to be wrought. The 'signs' spoken of are so many evidences that these are already at work. In brief time, therefore, we may reckon fully on seeing their fruit. Before that season is concluded, in fact, which begins with the 'buds,' we may reckon on seeing this 'fruit.' In other words, before the 'generation' is over that begins with the 'signs,' the things signified will have come. Not 'heaven' above, not 'earth' beneath, is so certain as this. Everything else is to 'pass away,' except 'these sayings of Mine.'

On the other hand, the exact 'day and hour' of their fulfilment is uncertain to every mind except One. This is why their fulfilment will come on those who live for the present only, with the same unexpected suddenness as the waters of the flood came on similar careless ones in the days of Noah. This also is why the result of their fulfilment shall be equally final and sharp. And why it is, finally, that I exhort all of you to be always on the 'watch.' 'Blessed is that servant,' who, because of this uncertainty and finality, only watches the more. His Master, when He cometh, shall make him ruler over all that He hath. But woe to that servant who, for the same reasons, banishes the thought from his heart. His Master's coming will hand him over to hopeless sorrow and shame.

The state of things at that time is so important that it deserves to be set forth under a different figure. 'Then shall the kingdom of heaven be likened' to a company of virgins at a marriage feast awaiting the bridegroom's approach. Although professing to be waiting, they will all be asleep, when first that approach is proclaimed ; moreover, fully half of their number, even when aroused, shall only be ready too late! In other words, not be 'ready' at all ; but for ever 'shut out.' To be watchful at all times is the only security for being ready at that!

Yet another parable may help to set forth this capital point. It is as though a ruler, going away from his own kingdom to 'another country' for a while, should 'call his own servants' and solemnly entrust them with such an amount of 'his goods' as they should be severally able to employ for him profitably during his absence. Naturally, on coming back, he reckons on finding them ready for him, with their accounts and results. Those who have dealt faithfully with their trust, whether comparatively little or great, will be openly commended and made welcome to a corresponding share in his joy. Those who have been unfaithful to their trust, on the other hand, however small its amount, will not be allowed to escape on that score. No 'unprofitable servant' must look at that time for anything less than total loss, and 'outer darkness,' and 'the weeping and gnashing of teeth.' If we would watch for Christ, we must work for Him too.

Last of all, besides watching and working, there must be patient waiting for Christ. The winding up of all things will shew all things in a light of its own. 'When the Son of Man shall come in His glory,' with 'all the angels' gathered around Him, and 'all the nations assembled' before Him, the history of these nations will be found, in reality, to have been a history of Himself. All neglected duties will prove to have been acts of hostility, all duties discharged will prove to have been acts of homage, to this representative

Man. The last thing suspected by most during the progress of Time, this will be the first thing taught by its close. Hence the utter astonishment, on both sides, of those who find it acted on then. Hence the sharp separation of those who are judged into two opposite flocks, the 'sheep' here on the right hand, and the 'goats' there on the left. Hence, also, the intensity of the welcome vouchsafed to the one, and the severity of the condemnation pronounced on the other. And hence, finally, both the depth and duration of the difference in their fates. 'These shall go away into eternal punishment: but the righteous into life eternal.'

With this awful description of His future manifestation as Judge of Time and Arbiter of Eternity, this comprehensive prophecy of Jesus of Nazareth is brought to its close.

CHAPTER VI.

THE EVE OF BETRAYAL.

Matt. xxvi. 1–30.

WHEN 'Jesus had finished all these sayings' respecting the things of the future, He brings His disciples suddenly back to the things of their time. 'Ye know that after two days is the feast of the Passover, and the Son of Man is betrayed to be crucified.' In every way the contrast is extreme. Over there is the sunny summit which is ultimately to be reached. Down below is the raging torrent which has immediately to be crossed.

A simultaneous, if not corresponding, contrast may be traced in the story. The Evangelist tells us less now of discourses than of significant deeds.

The first of these is something outside of Jesus, and on the part of His foes. 'The chief priests and rulers' assemble together in order to compass His death. They are moved to this by the nature of the claims advanced by Him now; and by the total failure of all their endeavours to overcome Him in words. They are hindered in it by the remarkable favour with which He is listened to by the people. Confessedly, it would be an exceedingly dangerous thing to lay hands on Him openly at that 'feast.' While they resolve, therefore, on seeking His life, they also resolve on taking care of their own. They are equally unscrupulous and prudent in their proceedings. They 'consult how they may take Jesus by subtilty,' and 'put Him to death.'

We may consider this His first contact with the shadow of death. Jesus is now a doomed man.

About this time, accordingly, we find Him treated as such in a very remarkable way. He is sitting as a guest in a house at Bethany belonging to 'Simon the leper.' A certain woman comes to Him there, having with her a precious alabaster vase, containing ointment of an equally precious description. The whole of this ointment, with lavish eagerness, she pours on His head. The action is observed with much disapproval by some who are there. 'How much better to have spent the price of this ointment in supplying the wants of the poor.' 'Not so at all,' replies the Master, reading their thoughts. 'On the contrary, instead of a blameable, she hath done a very good work. This exceptional time fully justifies this exceptional deed. In anointing Me thus, she has anointed one who in reality is as good as dead now. She has only done, in fact, what is done universally in preparing the bodies of men for the grave. Not even this gospel itself, therefore, in future days, shall be more widely known than this timely action of hers.

If this teaching of Jesus reached the understandings,

it did not touch the hearts, of all there. 'One of the twelve' (note this, to fathom rightly the deep enormity of the crime), 'named Judas Iscariot' (note this, not to put the disgrace of it on any head but that one), goes at once, or very soon after, to the chief priests, and voluntarily offers to arrange with them for the betrayal of his Master. This unlooked-for assistance is eagerly welcomed. The wicked compact is speedily made. Thirty miserable pieces of silver, the stipulated price of the crime, are paid over by them. The opportunity for committing it is watched for by him.

This is a second step in advance. The enemies of Jesus have found the means of accomplishing their purpose upon Him. He is more than 'doomed' now.

Apparently, also, this is now felt by Himself. His disciples come and ask His instructions respecting their Passover preparations. There is nothing beside this in their thoughts. But in His reply there is much beside, even the close proximity of His death. 'The Master saith, My time is at hand; I will keep the Passover at thy house with My disciples.'

A still greater solemnity marks His language when the eventide comes. The Passover has been duly prepared. They are all assembled together. It is now the midst of the feast. The Master's thoughts have gone forward from that scene to another which He knows to be close. Presently, He foretells it to them. 'Verily I say unto you, that one of you shall betray

Me.' Overwhelmed with sorrow, they say unto Him, one by one, 'Lord, is it I?' His reply, for the present, if not very direct, is explicit enough. 'He that dippeth his hand with Me in the dish, the same shall betray Me.' See, again, how awful the crime. See, also, how equally awful is the consequent doom. The bare thought of it, even with His own cross so near to Him, stirs the profoundest compassion of Christ. 'Woe unto that man by whom the Son of Man is betrayed! It had been good for that man if he had not been born!' If Judas *will* incur this doom, he shall not incur it unwarned! How still more awful, therefore, the silent calmness with which this warning is heard! 'Then Judas, which betrayed Him, answered and said, Master, is it I? He said unto him, Thou hast said.'

The sorrow of this night is a sorrow to be remembered for ever. With this object, certain memorable measures are now adopted by Christ. 'As they are eating,' He takes a portion of the unleavened bread which is on the table before Him. This He blesses and breaks, and proceeds to distribute to all who are there. Then, bidding them 'eat' it, He says to them, 'This is My body.' Afterwards, in a similar manner, He blesses and sets apart a portion of wine, saying, 'Drink ye all of it; for this is My blood of the New Testament, which is shed for many for the remission of sins.'

Much is meant by these actions and words.

On the one hand, they are a kind of rehearsal of the Saviour's imminent death. Like this bread and wine, so His body and blood are now to be broken and shed.

On the other, they are a gracious assurance of the unlimited efficacy of that death, in doing away with men's guilt. It is to avail for 'many'—even as many as will—'unto the remission of sins.' Finally, they teach, mystically, what is the appointed method of making that efficacy our own. That bread of life, that wine of agony, must be spiritually 'eaten' and 'drunk.'

A sudden light irradiates the darkness as the Saviour thinks of these truths. They lead His thoughts forward to another banquet, which is to have a triumphant 'wine' of its own. At that banquet all who partake of the heavenly food just provided by Him are to sit down. Not, however, until they shall all do so together, will He for His part taste again of 'this fruit of the vine.'

This solitary note of gladness and hope is followed by one of praise. They sing a hymn. Then the Saviour leaves that Passover chamber, and, accompanied by His disciples, goes forth to His fate.

CHAPTER VII.

THE NIGHT OF BETRAYAL.

Matt. xxvi. 31–75.

WHEN the disciples follow their Master from the Passover chamber to the Mount of Olives, they share His company, but hardly His thoughts. If they have begun to know at all what is to be done to Him, they know nothing yet of what is to be done by themselves. It is on this point, therefore, that He now specially cautions them in telling them, once more, of His death. As had long been predicted, so it would very soon be. 'All ye shall be offended because of Me this night: for it is written, I will smite the shepherd, and the sheep of the flock shall be scattered abroad.'

Yet, even so, He would not have them bereft of all hope. Though separated now, they shall meet again where they have met often before. 'After I am raised up, I will go before you into Galilee.' In every way, He sees farther than is seen by themselves.

One of them is greatly scandalised by what his Master has said. He can believe it of others, but not of himself. 'Though all men shall be offended because of Thee, yet will I never be offended.' Jesus, in reply, assures him that he will be so offended in

Him, that very night, as deliberately to renounce Him. 'Verily, I say unto thee, that this night, before the cock crow, thou shalt deny Me thrice.' Peter believes this even less. 'Even if I must die with Thee, yet will I not deny Thee.' The other disciples, following their leader, declare the same thing.

Little do they know of the storm that is coming to put their constancy to the test.

Their Master, therefore, who does know, does not rely on them much. Of the eleven disciples who accompany Him into the 'place called Gethsemane,' only three are taken with Him into its depths. 'Sit ye here,' He says to the rest, 'while I go yonder and pray.' Neither is it very much, when He *has* taken them, that He asks of those three:—little more, in fact, than some token of sympathy in the extremity of His grief. 'My soul is exceeding sorrowful, even unto death: tarry ye here, and watch with Me.' Even as much as this, moreover, though thus craved by Him, He fails to obtain. Going forward only 'a little,' as though to have His friends still within call, and falling 'on His face' to the ground, as though under the excessive weight of His anguish, His heart pours out this prayer: 'O My Father, if it be possible, let this cup pass away from Me: nevertheless, not as I will, but as Thou wilt.' Then, coming back, He finds His disciples buried in sleep. It is doubtful whether they are even aware of what He has said. Peter himself, who had talked of dying with Him, has proved unable to 'watch' with Him 'for one hour.' How chilling the sight! With all the willingness of their 'spirit,' with all the unspeakable tenderness of their Master as shewn by His recognising that willingness at that moment; such is the 'weakness' of the 'flesh,' that they have become wholly lost alike to His agony and their peril. He is utterly alone, therefore, when, for the second time, He departs and offers this prayer: 'O My Father, if this cup may not pass away from Me, except I drink it, Thy will be done.' Utterly alone, also, when again returning, He finds them still heavy in sleep. And utterly alone, finally, when, once more leaving them, He pours out once more the same prayer. *No one* hears it upon earth!

Yet what a supplication it is! What nameless horror; what determined purpose; what depth of submission; what height of confidence; what a world of mystery, it bespeaks! Why was such a request not granted at once? How came it to be presented at all? What a stern Judge, yet what a true 'Father!' What deep diversity of will, yet what deeper unity, we see here! Evidently secrets of the darkest nature lie at the root of this prayer.

One thing, however, with all its mystery, is unmistakeably clear. It has not been offered in vain. If it has not altogether removed that 'cup,' it has altered its taste. The midnight of anticipation is now over, if that of suffering has yet to be reached. Full and close, therefore, as this latter is now, it meets with nothing but steadiness in His gaze. 'Behold, the hour is at hand, and the Son of Man is betrayed into the hands of sinners. Rise, let us be going: behold, he is at hand that doth betray Me.'

As the words are spoken they are being fulfilled. 'Judas, one of the twelve'—a never-to-be-forgotten fact which helps both to aggravate, and, in a certain sense, to account for his crime—is seen approaching the spot. Behind him follows a great multitude armed with swords and staves. It is evident from whom they have come, viz., from the 'chief priests and elders of the people.' But why does this Judas come forward and salute his Master with such ostentatious and exuberant warmth? It is by this concerted signal that he directs the actions of the ignorant band. 'Whomsoever I shall kiss, that same is He; lay hold on *Him*.' How true he is to his bargain! How false to Christ!

Jesus understands the signal as well as the multitude. But, instead of opposing, He rather facilitates their evil design. 'Do that,' He says to Judas, 'for which thou art come.' (R.V.)

Forthwith, accordingly, the nefarious deed is accomplished: Jesus, at last, is in the hands of His foes.

Are there none to deliver Him from them?

Certainly, none upon earth. One of His disciples, indeed, makes an attempt—but it is a most harmful one—in that line. Neither, also, as things are, are there any in heaven. Multitudes, it is true, are standing there as though in battle array, who are both able and willing to intervene to good purpose, and who are waiting for nothing but the word of command. 'Thinkest thou that I cannot now pray to My Father, and He shall immediately give Me more than twelve legions of angels?' But, to His mind, there is an insuperable difficulty in the way of His asking that boon. He cannot say such words without unsaying others. He cannot speak these words without blotting out those. 'How then shall the *Scriptures* be fulfilled, that thus it must be?'

For all this, however, He feels the indignity with which He is treated. If His captors had wished to apprehend Him, why had they not done so as He sat in the Temple? Why come against Him as against a robber and in that place of seclusion, with swords and with staves? Yet here again He submits because He has submitted already to that higher force before-named. 'All this is done that the Scriptures of the prophets might be fulfilled.'

At this point, the fears of His disciples are too much for their faith. Supposing Him now to be forsaken by Himself, they 'forsake' Him as well.

More than ever, therefore, is He alone, when led away as a prisoner to where the Jewish Council are being hastily summoned to meet. One disciple, wishing to 'see the end,' has followed Him there a 'long way off,' and is now hoping to escape notice amongst the crowd of officials in the hall. But, except for *his* countenance, thus afraid to be seen, there is hardly a friendly face in the place. All the Council are bent unanimously on putting Jesus to death. With this object, they eagerly seek for witnesses who can bear witness against Him. After many failures, they find two who in some measure agree. 'This fellow said, I am able to destroy the temple of God, and build it in three days.' To this testimony, which Jesus seems to have regarded as amounting to nothing, He has nothing to say. The High Priest, however, proceeds to treat it as of the highest importance. Standing up, he expresses his astonishment (though without saying why) that it should be left without notice. 'Answerest Thou nothing? What is it which these witness against Thee?' To this appeal also, which simply left the previous testimony just where it was, Jesus again has nothing to say. The situation is growing perplexing to those who are seeking His death. If all their evidence comes to nothing, what is to be done? Perhaps they can obtain some admission from Himself, which can be turned to His ruin. Perhaps He can be made to bear witness against Himself, as it were. He is a lover of truth. They will appeal to His truth. He professes much piety. They will appeal to that too. In God's name, they will require Him to tell them what He really professes to be. 'I adjure Thee by the living God, that Thou tell us whether Thou be the Christ, the Son of God.'

To this question, thus put, and put by one in such a position of authority, Jesus at once and fully replies. Yes, He was the Christ. They had uttered the truth. And they should be made to know it too, in due time. 'Nevertheless I say unto you, Hereafter shall ye see the Son of Man sitting on the right hand of power, and coming in the clouds of heaven.'

Wild commotion arises immediately on hearing these words. The High Priest himself rends his garments, as though at their blasphemous sound. His ready assessors, without 'further witness,' agree to the verdict he asks. They 'answer' and say, 'He is guilty of death.' Many of those present then offer the grossest insults to the Saviour's person and claims. They 'spit in His face.' They 'buffet' Him. They smite Him with the palms of their hands. They defy Him even to name the hands by which He is struck. 'Prophesy unto us, Thou Christ, who is he that smote Thee?'

This to One who had just described Himself as the future Judge of mankind! What a depth of scorn! What a depth of forbearance! To all this storm of insult and outrage, not even a word!

Meanwhile, what has that disciple been doing who has followed Christ to that place? He has been trembling with fear lest his connection with Him should be believed in by those present. First, one accuses him of it; then, another. He denies it to both. He does so the second time with an oath.

Notwithstanding this, the accusation is repeated by some of them that stand by. The very dialect in which he denies it helps to establish its truth. 'Surely thou also art one of them: for thy speech bewrayeth thee.' Terrified at this, he plunges deeper into the waters of sin. He begins to 'curse and to swear.' So far from being intimate with Jesus of Nazareth, he does not even possess His acquaintance. 'I do not know the Man!' he cries out. As he says so, the 'cock crows.' A sudden light, which is not that of the morning, flashes immediately on his soul. He sees where he was; and where he is now; what he promised; what he has done! And he rushes out to hide the weeping which he cannot restrain.

This disgraced disciple, this timid heart, this fainting spirit, this broken reed, is the best earthly support —if not, indeed, the only earthly support—of Jesus of Nazareth on that infamous night!

CHAPTER VIII.

UNSULLIED INNOCENCE.

Matt. xxvii. 1-26.

By the time that the 'morning' has fully 'come,' it finds those who had sentenced Jesus of Nazareth to death consulting together as to the best means of carrying out their design. They finally resolve on handing Him over to the authority of Pontius Pilate, the Roman governor, in whose hands, at that time, the power of death seems to have lain. And they proceed to take Jesus, .for this purpose, to the governor's house.

The significance of this proceeding is not lost on that unhappy disciple who has put Christ in their power. What he had expected his treachery to lead to, beyond some immediate pecuniary gain to himself, we are not informed. It is highly probable that the overpowering spirit of avarice had hitherto banished such thoughts from his mind. But what is now signified by this public binding of Jesus of Nazareth, and leading Him away as a captive to the Roman governor's house, he sees only too well. As to his Master, it means that they have condemned Him to death. As to himself, it signifies that he has helped forward that crime.

Filled, in consequence, with horror and shame, he desires, if it may be, even now, to prevent the accomplishment of their plan. Cost what it may, he will do this, if he possibly can. Cost what it may, both in money and shame, he will do this, if he can. Take back your bribe; take back the whole of it—so he says in effect. I acknowledge openly that I ought never to have touched it, knowing all that I know. I have sinned! Yes, I have sinned outrageously! 'I have betrayed innocent blood!'

What a confession! What a confession from so close a companion! From so suspicious a nature! From such a covetous heart! At such a critical time! It is like the whitest of lights on a statue of alabaster on the blackest of nights!

Also, what a merciful warning! If only these priests will give it due heed; if only they will listen to this spontaneous evidence with as much anxiety as they manifested a little while ago in seeking for false witness; they may even yet be held back.

As it is, however, they remain as determined as though it had never been heard. Neither the misery of Judas, nor yet the cause of it, has any effect upon them. Be it so that he has indeed been guilty of betraying—none the less are they prepared for shedding—innocent blood. To their hardened souls, such a reflection is of no moment at all. 'What is that to us? See thou to that.'

Even thus repulsed, the unhappy traitor cannot

acquiesce in their deed. If *they* will not take, *he* cannot keep, the price of his guilt. Flinging it down, therefore, he flies away from it, as from something accursed. Afterwards, it comes to light that this is not all. Unable to deliver that innocent life, he puts an end to his own. See the profound effect which the innocence of Jesus has produced on this wicked man's heart. He cannot live—and see it condemned!

Meanwhile, the men who had bribed him remain undisturbed still. Carefully gathering together the miserable pieces of silver which he had flung down, their only anxiety now is how to invest them in the most politic way. As the price of blood, it would be too scandalous a proceeding to return them to the treasury of the Temple. On the other hand, it would be just as absurd, in their judgment, to turn them to no profit at all. What is ultimately done is to employ them in purchasing a piece of ground in the near neighbourhood of the city, which had been formerly used as a potter's field, but which was now probably in an exhausted condition, and so to be had for the exact sum of which they had to dispose. Not impossibly, they knew of this through Judas himself. One of the principal reasons, in fact, for his demanding and accepting that exact sum as a bribe, may have been his discovery that it would exactly enable him to purchase that field. Anyhow, if the transaction was begun by him, it is completed by them. Thinking the place a convenient one 'to bury strangers in'

—and looking upon it, there is little doubt, as quite good enough too for such a purpose,— they purchase it for that use.

The step turns out a momentous one in regard to the future. That field becomes a notorious one in the history of mankind. Bought with the money which even dying Judas refused to keep because of its being the price of innocent blood, it has ever since been identified with that fact. It is 'the field of blood to this day.'

The step proves, also, to be not less momentous with regard to the past. Either as a thing of vision, or else of typical fact, certain language in one of the prophets relates the purchase of an exactly similar field at an exactly identical price; and describes that price also as being, in some way, the value set on a life. 'They took the thirty pieces of silver, the price of him that was valued, whom they of the children of Israel did value; and gave them for the potter's field, as the Lord appointed me.'

It was a mysterious, and yet a plain, foreshadowing of what has now taken place. This very field had long been destined to testify to the innocency of Jesus. Whatever else is doubtful, this truth is clear, in this prophetical word.

The chief priests have now arrived at the governor's house, and have placed their Prisoner before him. Pilate looks on Him, and can hardly believe in the seriousness of the charges he hears. 'Thou the King of the Jews? Dost Thou really call Thyself by that name?'

As the governor, in asking this question, is only endeavouring to do his duty, the answer given is immediate and clear. 'It is as thou sayest. I do.'

A whirlwind of accusation from the Jewish rulers follows these words.

Jesus gives it no heed. He is so silent, in fact, that His examiner begins to question whether He is quite in possession of His senses. 'Hearest Thou not how many things they witness against Thee?'

Still never a word.

The astonishment of the governor passes all bounds. There is some awe in it too. This unaccountable silence is more eloquent than any number of words. What is to be done?

It was the custom at that feast for those in authority to gratify the multitudes then collected together, by giving liberty to some one prisoner, 'whomsoever they would.' Perhaps this custom can be so handled now as to set this prisoner free. A notable prisoner, of the name of Barabbas, is lying in prison. It is well known that he is lying there for a most flagitious offence. This 'Jesus,' on the contrary, has been delivered up for envy alone. I will offer to the multitude to give liberty to one of these two. Put to them thus, they cannot hesitate long. They will allow 'Barabbas' to remain in prison. They will call for 'Jesus' instead.

Whilst Pilate is considering how to carry this out—

or just, it may be, as he is in the act of mooting it first —an unexpected voice comes to his ear. During the previous night, or early that morning, his 'wife' has had a dream about Christ. The details of that dream are not told us; but its effect speaks for itself. She has been so scared by it that she sends her husband word of it, even whilst seated in court. She even dares, in consequence, to entreat and admonish him as to his conduct while there. 'Have thou nothing to do, I beseech thee, with condemning that just man who is at present before thee. Only this very day I have been shewn the peril of doing so in a most terrible dream.'

This is another singular, but striking testimony in the same line as before. Even sleeping eyes are made to see the innocency of Jesus.

It is another merciful message, also, in the same line as before. Dreams and omens to Roman ears were as signs from above. It is in their language, therefore, at this crucial moment, that this Roman governor is thus graciously warned.

There are voices, however, of a different sort which now prevail with him more. After receiving his wife's message, he proceeds with the plan devised by him for delivering Jesus. But the Jewish rulers seem to have taken advantage of the delay. At any rate, when he puts the proposed question, he fails of the answer he sought. The people have been 'persuaded' to ask the wrong man. More than that, to his great disappointment, they ask the death of the right. Do they understand their own words? To make quite sure on this point, he determines to put the question to them in a more definite shape. '*Which* of the two shall I free?' They are just as definite in reply. 'They say unto him, Barabbas.' Still doubting, he desires to put to them strongly the other side of the question. 'What shall I do, then, with Jesus which is called the Christ?' They return answer again—they 'all' of them do—'let Him go to the cross.' Much shocked at this, he remonstrates vehemently against so grievous a wrong. '*Why* should this be? Shew me *cause* for it! What "evil" justifies so extreme a demand?' To this remonstrance—having no reason to offer—they only reply by their cries. 'Let Him be crucified! Let Him be crucified! Σταυρωθήτω. Let Him die on the cross.' In all that sea of faces, every tossing wave seems to be foaming white with that cry!

In the presence of such a 'tumult,' it seems to Pilate that there is only one thing he can do. Calling for water, he washes his hands in it, in the presence of all. He explains, also, what he means by this, in the hearing of all. 'I am innocent of the blood of this just person. That must rest upon you.'

It is a final testimony, and a transcendent one, to the innocency of Jesus. Like the disciple who betrayed Him, so the judge who condemns Him, condemns himself for so doing. 'I am consenting to that which I hereby acknowledge to be an inexcusable wrong.'

It is also a final and merciful warning to those Jewish rulers who are bent on His death. They are demanding that from which even a heathen tyrant shrinks in horror and fear!

Yet this message also—like those before it—is without effect on their hearts. Notwithstanding all that Pilate has said and done, they move the people to defy the uttermost consequences of the step they are taking. 'Then answered all the people and said, His blood be on us and on our children!'

Pilate himself, also, takes the same consequences, after all, on himself. He gives the order for that decisive double step which insures the consummation of all. He sets the guilty man free. He puts the innocent man in his place. 'Then released he Barabbas unto them; and when he had scourged Jesus, he delivered Him to be crucified.'

What a picture! What a result! The Holy Jesus handed over to a murderer's doom!'

CHAPTER IX.

INSCRUTABLE DEPTHS.

Matt. xxvii. 27-56.

THE action of Pilate has placed Jesus in the cruel hands of those iron legionaries who have conquered the world. True to their character, they take a brutal delight in their horrible task. To their minds the whole process entrusted to them is a matter of sport; one, therefore, in which the 'whole cohort' must be invited to join. In this spirit the assembled soldiers first deprive their unresisting Prisoner of His usual outermost garment; and then invest Him, by way of mockery, with a scarlet one in its stead. In the same spirit, they either weave together a crown of thorns, or take one already woven, and hrust it on to His head. After this they place in His hands a feeble sceptre of reed; and offer to Him, in contempt, the outward homage of body and lip, 'bowing the knee and saying to Him, Hail, King of the Jews!' What a pleasure it is—what a safe pleasure—to insult that silent Man thus! What shouts of derision cause that 'common hall' to ring again with their sound! Did you ever see such a King? such a sceptre? such a beggarly crown?

Soon, however, these indirect outrages begin to weary upon them. All the sooner, perhaps, because in this instance they so completely fail of their mark. It is provoking to find that these insults have not provoked Him even into a look of complaint. Grosser insolence, therefore, and more direct outrages, are resorted to next. Some of these tormentors of Jesus even go so far as to spit in His face, as though to shew their contempt for His person. Others among them, by way of shewing the same unmeasured contempt for His claims, plucking away the poor symbol of authority which they had placed in His hands, turn it as it were against its bearer, and smite Him therewith ' on the head.' Even these things, however, in the case of this Sufferer, begin, in turn, to grow stale. He can endure more—in this way also—than they can inflict. At last, therefore, they begin to think it time for the direst outrage of all. So stripping off that garment of scarlet which they had kept on Him till now, and replacing it by His own, they lay on His shoulders His own instrument of torture (as appears to have been customary in all similar cases), and proceed to lead Him away.

They do not lead Him, thus burdened, very far before making a change. As they 'come out,' a native of Cyrene, Simon by name, happens to come in their way. Him, as they have power to do, they at once ' impress,' in order to make him carry Christ's cross. Is this due to a solitary touch of pity for Jesus on the part of these men? Or is it only an indication, on their part, of impatience and haste? In either case, on the part of Jesus Himself, it is a most significant change. It proves how deeply He has felt, though He has never resented, all He has had to go through.

Arrived, in time, at the place of execution—known as Golgotha, or the place of a skull—some one offers Him a cup of wine mingled with gall. This is done, it is thought, in order to give Him strength to endure the pains of the cross; or else, it may be, in order to render Him less sensitive to them. In either case, while He respects the offer, He does not avail Himself of it. He will not borrow strength, nor will He accept assuagement, in bearing the sufferings of that hour. Nothing must take away from that cup of sorrow which He has to drink to its dregs. This other cup, therefore, is only tasted, and then put to one side.

The terrible process of the crucifixion itself is left undescribed in this story. Partly, perhaps, because the bare fact is more than enough for our thoughts. 'THEY CRUCIFY HIM.' What a portent is this! Nothing happens to prevent the wreaking of this unspeakable wrong! Much is done, as we have seen, to demonstrate the innocence, nothing is done to protect the person, of this King of the Jews! *He* chooses, and God allows Him, to be made a crucified Man! Was there ever an event to stir us up to greater searchings of heart?

The surroundings of this central fact are such as to give it greater emphasis still. Below and in front of the crucified Jesus are the Roman soldiers, busily engaged in dividing His garments by lot, thus fulfilling exactly, however unconsciously, what the Psalmist had said: 'They parted My garments among them, and upon My vesture did they cast lots.' Above His head we see affixed the customary 'accusation;' or rather, perhaps, we ought to say, what is meant to be such. For the inscription amounts, in fact, instead of this, to a verbal acknowledgment of His claims. 'This is Jesus the King of the Jews.' On either side of Him are other crosses, with convicted felons upon them. Can we not see at once, if we see at all, how much it all means? An acknowledged King is numbered with malefactors! Perfect innocence is dying as guilt!

The spectators at the time, however, with their blinded minds, understand nothing of this. In all this mystery they see nothing calling for either compassion or fear. The ordinary 'passers-by,' for example, of whom of course there are multitudes at this festival season, openly treat this crucified Jesus with almost sportive contempt. Wagging their heads, they call out to Him thus: 'Thou that destroyest the Temple, and buildest it in three days, save Thyself: if Thou *art* the Son of God, come down from the cross.' The Jewish rulers, also, who ought to have been leaders in good, are at least equally blind. They seem, in fact, to be even more indecent in their exultation and hate. 'He saved others, Himself He cannot save. If He be the King of Israel, let Him come down now from the cross, and we will believe Him. He trusted in God; let Him deliver Him now, if He will have Him: for He said, I am the Son of God.' The wretched thieves, also, who are crucified with Him, cast the same in His teeth. At this moment, in short, He hears nothing whatever from human voices but bitter hatred and scorn. A trial, probably, as great in its way as crucifixion itself. A trial, if so, which would exactly double the severity of its pangs.

A source of even deeper distress is hinted at next. A pall of darkness overshadows the land from the sixth hour to the ninth. It is under that darkness that Jesus battles with this additional grief. It seems a perplexity to some extent to Himself. The cry which it elicits is an undoubted astonishment to him who is telling this story. Hence, both the time and manner of its utterance, and the identical sounds also of which it consisted, and the meaning also which they conveyed to the ear, are all told us in turn. 'About the ninth hour Jesus cried with a loud voice, saying, Eli, Eli, lama sabachthani? that is to say, My God, My God, why hast Thou forsaken Me?'

Mysterious indeed are the words!

'Why hast Thou forsaken *Me*?' *Me*, the innocent Jesus? *Me*, with whom Thou hast declared Thyself to be always well pleased?

'Why,' also, 'hast Thou *forsaken* Me?' In what sense, to what extent, on what account, is this true? What is actually being done, on the one hand—what is actually being endured, on the other—to call forth such a complaint? To call it forth, above all, from those long-suffering lips? These things are not explained to us here. We are only bidden to ponder them in wonder and grief. A more pathetic utterance—a more astounding utterance—never came from man's heart.

Part of its pathos seems to penetrate to some who are there. To the dull hearing of one bystander, at any rate, that cry of distress is a cry for help to Elias—an evidence of delirium brought about by excess of bodily pain. Accordingly, he seeks to allay this by the best means in his power. Putting a sponge full of vinegar on the end of a reed, he endeavours therewith to apply it to the Sufferer's lips. The other bystanders remonstrate with him, and bid him desist. Possibly, they are at last beginning to suspect something of the unusual character of the scene. 'Let be,' they say; let us wait the result; let us see whether Elias *will* come to give this man help.

While the attention of all is thus concentrated on the suffering Jesus, He cries out again.

This time His utterance, strangely enough, speaks both of victory and of death. 'Jesus, when He has cried again with a loud voice, dismisses His spirit.'

Immediately that cry is replied to in the neighbouring Temple of God. The jealous privacy of long generations is suddenly gone. The heavy 'vail,' which, for ages past, had only just permitted the annual passage of the blood-besprinkled high priest to the glory beyond it, is a means of separation no longer. Like the body of Jesus, it is rent in twain from the top to the bottom.

A similar reply is also given among the rocks of the earth. Their solid strength is torn asunder by the power of that voice.

A third reply is heard next among the homes of the dead. 'The graves are opened, and many bodies of the saints which are sleeping there arise, and come (afterwards) into the Holy City, and appear unto many.'

A final reply, and a most significant one, comes from the hearts of the living. In the early part of that day, numberless voices had scouted the idea of that crucified man being God's Son. Later on, it almost *seemed* as though He had begun to doubt it Himself. Now it is proclaimed by the very voice which had given the command for His death. Cæsar it was in reality, in the person of Pilate, who ordered that crime. Cæsar it is now, by Pilate's deputy, who confesses this truth. 'When the centurion, and they that are with him, watching Jesus, see the earthquake and these things that are done, they fear greatly, saying aloud, Truly this *was* God's Son!'

Thus does imperial Rome do unconscious homage to this dead 'King of the Jews!'

All this, however, instead of explaining, increases the difficulty before us. If it be so marvellous a thing to see such innocency delivered to death, it is almost more so to see such omnipotence submitting thereto. Is this saying too much? What amazing majesty, what kingly authority, what superhuman power, have been nailed to that cross! Possibly, some such thoughts may be perplexing the minds of those faithful 'women' who are described here as 'beholding' all 'afar off;' and who are also said to have 'followed Jesus out of Galilee, ministering unto Him; amongst them being such as Mary Magdalene, and Mary the mother of James and Joses, and the mother of Zebedee's children.' Certainly, we who read the account, though standing, in one sense, farther off still, cannot escape from such thoughts. What commanding weakness! What awe-inspiring meekness! What dying energy we see here! Who is this that, in submitting to death, overcomes it as well? Who is this, that restores life to others in the act of 'dismissing' His own?

The Evangelist does not directly inform us how to answer these questions. He simply bids us behold, in this death of Jesus, the most astounding of facts!

CHAPTER X.

TOTAL ECLIPSE.

Matt. xxvii. 57–66.

THE mystery attaching to the death of Jesus does not interfere with its truth. Difficult to account for, it is even more difficult—it is impossible—to deny.

The next transaction of which our history informs us gives plain evidence of this fact. A certain man of substance and standing, known as Joseph of Arimathæa, is in Jerusalem at this time. Although a sincere disciple of the now crucified Jesus, he appears to be in such a position as to have ready access to the governor's presence. He goes to him accordingly, and asks permission to take down the body of Christ. Pilate consents, and gives the requisite orders for having it delivered to his care. Plain proof, of course, that, in the eyes of them both, it is now a body without life. Neither would Joseph have asked it, nor would Pilate have delivered it, unless fully assured on this point.

The way in which Joseph deals with his trust gives further evidence in this line. Under his supervision, a fair linen cloth is wrapped round the length of the body of Jesus with reverent care. With equal reverence and care that body is then laid in a new sepulchre, which the same Joseph had caused to be prepared for himself in the solid rock of that spot. And a similar or even greater degree of care is next exhibited in closing that sepulchre up; a 'stone' of apparently unusual magnitude being used for that purpose. On this point we may judge perhaps from one expression employed. Notwithstanding the lateness of the hour (for 'the even was come'), and the consequent need of the most urgent despatch, if they would avoid infringing on the sanctity of the rapidly approaching commencement of the Sabbath day, that stone is not carried, but 'rolled' to its place.

These things, of course, prove not only the presence, but the undoubted presence, of death. Just that which is always done for the undeniably dead is done in this case. Only it is done, it would seem, with unusual carefulness, because of the unusual character of the loss. Its significance, therefore, cannot be missed. Those linen wrappings, so unfitted for motion, that hallowed sepulchre, only fitted for rest, and the extra precautions so anxiously taken for protecting that which is deposited there, all proclaim the same truth. Joseph has buried there the very idea of Christ's still being alive.

Others, also, have been 'sitting by' and doing much the same thing. Two, at least, of those women who had watched the crucifixion of Jesus afar off, have now watched His interment as well. If they have not personally assisted, they have fully acquiesced, in all that Joseph has done. To them also, the only place for the body of Jesus now is the place of the dead.

There is nothing less, in fact, than an accumulation of evidence in regard to this point. It is a matter on which even the enemies of Jesus are at one with His friends. 'The Chief Priests and the Pharisees gather together' in order to speak to Pilate once more about Christ. But their manner of doing so is widely different from what it had been only some short time before. To their apprehension all that is left of Jesus now requiring to be attended to, is the mere memory of His words. 'Sir, we remember that that deceiver said, while He was yet alive, After three days I will rise again.' And even this memory appears to them to be deserving of attention only in connection with other men's acts. Only if the 'disciples' of Jesus were to come and 'steal His body away,' and then 'say to the people' that He had risen from the dead, need there be cause for alarm. In that case, no doubt, the 'last error,' as they deemed it to be, might be 'worse than the first.' But excepting so, they know of nothing else to cause even a shadow of fear. Protect us from this contingency—such is the meaning of their language to the governor—and you protect us from all.

Pilate's almost contemptuous reply—as though he despised their fears in his heart—is all they wish for in other respects. 'Take the guard you desire. Go to the sepulchre. Make everything safe.' They go willingly; and endeavour to do so in every conceivable way. To the security afforded by the extraordinary magnitude of the stone by which the mouth of the sepulchre is closed up, they add that of a 'seal.' To this second security they then add a third, securer than both. A detachment of Roman soldiers, in all probability the best class of sentinels ever seen among men, is stationed there as a guard. A guard, be it observed also, against a danger of the flimsiest possible kind! Who are these that are suspected of robbing that sepulchre of the body of Jesus? Those that deserted Him while alive.

Altogether, therefore, how undeniable here is the absolute absence of life! We have followed this 'Christ' till we have seen Him crucified, and laid in this tomb. We have followed His cause, till His enemies believe that they have buried that too. Their last fear respecting it amounts to little more than a jest. And against this, as we have seen, they have protected themselves by an absurdly excessive defence. Jesus is dead; and His influence too. So those Roman sentinels are proclaiming to the world, as they keep guard by that tomb.

PART V.

THE RE-APPEARANCE OF CHRIST.

CHAPTER I.

A DOUBLE DAWN.

Matt. xxviii. 1–10.

THE Sabbath Day during which the Roman soldiers had been appointed to guard the sepulchre of Jesus comes to its close. The shadows of evening cover the land. The hours of night have begun.

By and by the day-break is about to appear. The slight general stir, like that of a person on the point of awaking, which usually characterises that juncture, is accompanied in this case by indications of movement of a more definite kind. Certain distant figures— figures undoubtedly in motion, whatever their nature —are just discernible in the dark. Presently, as the darkness is mitigated, and their movements continue, these figures are seen to be approaching the guard. Soon after, it is possible to distinguish them as the figures of women; even of the same women, in fact, as some of those of whom we have twice before heard. Yonder figure, for example, is certainly that of 'Mary of Magdala.' And that figure, near her, is that of the 'other Mary,' who was with her before. It is now evident, also, that they are approaching for the purpose of 'seeing the sepulchre' of Jesus. Their whole aspect shews that that saddest of pleasures is the outside of their hopes.

At this point the scene of the story suddenly shifts. We are no longer with the soldiers at the sepulchre, seeing the women approach. We are with the women themselves, on the way to it, trying to see its true place. They do see it at last, as they saw it before, in the side of the rock. They see also, in its immediate neighbourhood, the forms of the guard. So much as this, in the waning darkness—so much too much, to those sorrowing hearts!—it is possible to make out.

But what is this which is under no necessity of being 'made out?' What is this which these women 'behold,' as by a light of its own? The solid earth is trembling violently under their feet. A form is descending which is seen at once to be that of an angel of God. He is at the sepulchre. He has rolled back the stone. He is seated upon it. See his countenance—it is like the 'lightning.' See his 'raiment'—'as white as snow.' See, also, the effects of his presence. Those Roman soldiers, the terror of the nations, have become as 'dead men.' And even the all-absorbing grief of the women themselves is half-forgotten in fear.

Their fear is seen and noticed immediately by the angel of God. He sees very much more. He sees the purpose for which they have come. He understands exactly the cause of their sorrow. Even the difficulty which they will experience in receiving the consolation which he is about to offer them, he comprehends, and removes. 'Fear not ye,' as these do, who are here for a different purpose. '*Ye* seek Jesus, I know, which was crucified.' Well, 'He is *not* here,' now. 'He has risen again, as He said.' And lo ! here is demonstration that, at any rate, He is not here now. Come and see where He lay.

These combined influences begin to tell on the minds of the women. Astonishing as is the announcement just made to them, the utter falsehood of it would be to them more astonishing still. With such authority, and such recollections, and such positive proof behind that announcement, how can it be false? Thus gradually are they waking up to a sense of its truth.

That being so, they can now be entrusted—and the trust itself will assist greatly in confirming their faith—to tell the story in turn. Also, it being so joyful a story, they cannot tell it too soon. Also, being so wondrous a story, they are authorised to promise, when they do tell it, further proof of its truth. 'Go quickly, and tell His disciples that He is risen from the dead. Tell them also that He is going before you into Galilee, and that there ye shall see Him. Tell them all this, for I have told it to you, and ye may rely on my word.'

Thus exhorted, these faithful women are very soon gone. Fear and joy unite together to quicken their steps. Every moment that empty sepulchre is left farther behind. What sights they have seen! What things they have heard! What solemn tidings, what joyful intelligence, they have to make known! Oh! for wings to reach those they desire! Oh! for breath to tell all!

Suddenly, instead of flying, they are standing transfixed. Can it be? Yes, it must be! It is the Master Himself! His own aspect! His own voice! His own greeting once more! And yet, withal, is He *quite* the same as when they saw Him before? Is there not a perceptible change in them, which is as it were the reflection of the change which they see in Himself? Why else do we now behold them 'worshipping' Him on their faces? Why else do we see them now 'embracing His feet?' With no less affection, there is a deeper awe, than ever before.

Probably the marked graciousness of the words which He now speaks is in order to temper this awe.

To the women themselves—as He had said before to His disciples both on the Mount of Transfiguration and on the Sea of Galilee, on two occasions which were analogous to this to a certain extent—even so He says now—'Be not afraid.'

To those eleven 'disciples' who had forsaken Him on His trial, He is more considerate still. He at once anticipates and dispels their fears by the message He sends. If He fully remembers, He shews also that He has fully forgiven the past. 'Go, tell My *brethren*, that they go into Galilee,' where they have so often seen Me before; and that there 'they shall see Me again.'

Was this meant to imply that He would restore them there to the Apostleship they had lost? It was certainly meant to signify that that future meeting would be full of promise and hope.

Meantime, this renewed promise of it has already done much. For those commissioned to carry this message it has already done much. From the minds of these first human witnesses of the Resurrection of Christ it has banished the last shadow of doubt. By this gracious word of His, they know for certain that He has risen again. Yonder just-risen sun itself is not plainer now to their eyes than is this truth of truths to their minds!

CHAPTER II.

AN IMPOSSIBLE STORY.

Matt. xxviii. 11-15.

By the time that the guards at the sepulchre have recovered their senses, the scene there is much changed. The angel has vanished. The earthquake is over. If the women can still be seen going away in the distance, that appears to be all. Nothing but an open and emptied sepulchre remains in sight on the spot. What is to be done?

What ought to be done is patent enough. The singular significance of that silent testimony ought to be carefully weighed. To all persons able to understand the language of facts, it signifies much. To those appointed for the express purpose of preventing the kind of thing which has now come to pass, it signifies more. It signifies that they have been face to face with a greater power than their own. It signifies, also, that they have been defeated by it with almost contemptible ease. Without inflicting a wound, or striking a blow, or even speaking a syllable, their keen weapons and disciplined skill and proverbial vigilance and unquestioned courage have been put hopelessly to the worse. A completer victory was never obtained even over the weakest of foes. The defeat is at once of the uttermost, and of the most irreversible, kind.

Men thus defeated—fighting men thus defeated, especially—ought to lay the lesson to heart. Who was this, the mere sight of whom had caused them to become as dead men? How was it also that such a being went no farther than this? And who, above all, was that other One for whom he interfered thus? What a significant warning, what a merciful escape, as well as what a signal defeat, they have had! It required an effort—surely a great effort—to put such considerations aside.

Some of the soldiers are equal to it, if others are not. The inertia of unbelief proves too much in their case—as it does in so many others—even for the impact of facts. As these men recover their senses, they also recover their hardness of heart. The departed danger is gradually forgotten in the thought of that which remains. That the body of Jesus has disappeared does not admit of a doubt. This will soon be known to those who commissioned them to keep watch at that spot. Would it not be wise to anticipate the inquiries which will certainly follow? Had they not better give their own account of that which has happened? and give it, also, at once?

Those who have reasoned in this manner act in accordance. They 'go into the city;' they find out the chief priests; they inform them of 'all.'

The first result is altogether to confound those who first hear the report. By themselves, in fact, these 'Chief Priests' feel so unable to decide on the proper measures to be adopted, that they hastily summon the 'Elders' also to confer with them on the subject. A solemn and anxious council is held. Evidently, they have heard of that of which they had never previously dreamt!

The next result is to silence these rulers in a most extraordinary manner. Defeated soldiers generally come in for abundance of blame, more especially on the part of those who have been led to rely on their help. Even if such persons do not reproach them directly and in so many words, they do so tacitly by expecting them to try and recover the day. Can you not restore matters by another attempt? It is to be especially noted, therefore, that we hear of nothing similar in this case of defeat. Though doubtless disappointed almost to madness by the course of events, not a whisper of blame is heard falling from the lips of the priests. Neither, in all their perplexity, does it seem to occur to them to suggest remedial steps. Evidently, the story told them has not been of a character to encourage such thoughts. The strongest of men may be excused for succumbing to a power above man's! The bravest of men must not be called upon to face it again!

The final result is to drive these rulers to still more singular *speech*. Although they dare not ask the soldiers to *act* as though their report was untrue, they deliberately determine, for their own part, to speak of it as false. And, what is more, they ask the soldiers also to speak of it as false. 'The tale which you have now told us you must never repeat. You must say, instead, that "His disciples came by night and stole Him away while you slept."'

It is a bold course, not to say, a brazen one; yet desperate, too.

For it is asking men, first, to say that which they know to be false; and so to *shew* that they cannot be trusted to do the thing they are asked!

It is asking them, also, to tell a falsehood which reflects the grossest disgrace on themselves. What business had they to be 'asleep' at all when appointed to 'watch?'

A falsehood, further, which will inevitably involve them in the greatest personal risk. To a Roman legionary it was certain death to be found asleep at his post.

A falsehood, finally, of such a construction, as to lack even the appearance of truth. Can *sleeping* watchmen tell us of *anything* except their own *dreams?*

These considerations appear to be weighed deeply on both sides of the case. On the one hand, they account for the magnitude of the bribe demanded by the soldiers. On the other, they account for the strange willingness of the Jewish rulers to pay it. In their extremity they even do more. They use language which sounds like a pledge to bribe Pilate himself, if need be. 'If this come to a hearing before the governor, we will persuade him, and secure you.'

This last argument is a conclusive one to the minds of the soldiers. Knowing what they do of the cupidity of the governor, and seeing what they do of the terror of the rulers, they at last believe themselves safe in consenting to accept the offer before them. Nothing, consequently, remains now but to carry the compact out. They 'take' this 'large money' as a sufficient counterpoise even for such a monstrous request. Then, money in hand, they go forth, and 'do as they are taught.'

Others, next, hearing them, repeat the same tale.

Years afterwards, in fact — even as many years after as the date of the composition of this Gospel itself—those who thus denied the truth of Christ's rising again, are still found 'reporting' to others this same impossible tale.

A convincing proof that they have found nothing better to put in its place.

CHAPTER III.

AN ETERNAL WORK.

Matt. xxviii. 16-20.

CHRIST has risen again. Even the subterfuges of those who hate Him declare this to be true. The crucified Jesus is a living Man—a living Teacher—once more. What is to ensue?

The answer is given at that critical meeting in distant Galilee of which we have thrice before heard. Both previous to His death and since His rising again, both by His own voice and by that of the angel, He had appointed that part of the land of Israel for a special interview with His own. It now comes out, that He had also selected the precise spot in that land where He would meet them again. Either because it was more convenient to them, or more sequestered in situation, or in some other way better fitted for the meeting proposed, one 'mountain' among the mountains of Galilee had been 'appointed' for this end. A touch of definiteness as to *place*, which serves to shew the marked definiteness of the *purpose* in view.

Thither, accordingly, on the proper day, 'the eleven disciples' proceed. This definiteness of *number* seems to intimate that they are there by themselves; or, if others are with them, that they are only so as a kind of appendage to them. Out of the original 'twelve' the one traitor has gone. The remaining eleven, now that their Master has died and risen again, have come here, by His own special appointment, to meet Him again. Why is this, unless because He has something special to communicate to them? It does not follow, of necessity, that it is something exclusive as well.

We cannot be sure of the same definiteness in regard to the appointed hour of assembling. The Saviour may have told His disciples to come together *about* such a time of the day, wishing them to be ready for Him whenever He came. Or He may, perhaps, have appointed them a definite hour; and they may have anticipated it in their natural anxiety to avoid being too late. Either way, He is not with them when we see them at first.

By and by, however, so it is written, they 'see Him' approach. They all 'see Him,' but not all in the same manner at first. Some among them, with keener vision or stronger faith than the rest, recognise Him at once, and immediately are on their faces adoring His presence. Others among them, until He is close, feel in some uncertainty still. They are too perturbed as yet, or too anxious, to be without any measure of doubt. It is a time of suspense, and of much interest too. These early disciples are not mere enthusiasts, led away by their hopes. Their personal belief is not a contagion, caught from those they are with. All the more, therefore, when they do believe, may we believe in them too. 'Dubitatum est ab illis, ne dubitaretur a nobis.'

By the time that the light of the Master's presence is fully among them, the doubts of all have all gone. What they now need, therefore, is to be assured fully, not of His identity, but His power. Vast is the difference, in this respect, between the present time and the past. He had been with them before, if not exactly in weakness, yet in subjection and shame. As He had said Himself, and as all His history then had made plain, He had come, 'not to be ministered unto, but to minister,' and even to be subject to others, so far as to give His life a 'ransom for many.' But that condition of things is all over, now that that 'ransom' is over. He has not risen again to be a servant, but to be a ruler and judge. This is the point which He now wishes them to understand to the full. Everything needed for this new description of function—everything needed both above and below—has been placed now in His hands. 'All authority hath been given unto Me in heaven and on earth.'

Some of the authority thus put upon Him He puts next upon them. As His first disciples, He commissions them to make disciples of others. He commissions them also to do this in all parts of the earth. 'Go ye and make disciples of all nations.' What a glorious task! What an ample charter! How extensive a field! This is calling them to be Apostles afresh! to be Apostles indeed!

What shall they teach men to believe—what shall they teach men to observe—what are they themselves to look for—in going forth to this work?

A form of sound words is given in answer to the first of these questions, which is equally simple and deep. On the one hand, it is such as to correspond perfectly (though not a little mysteriously also) with the new position of Christ. On the other hand, it is such as to comprise in it everything that He would have men called upon to believe. His messengers are to 'baptize' men 'in the Name of the Father, and of the Son, and of the Holy Ghost.' Only those are to be acknowledged as His disciples who acknowledge the doctrines involved in those words. That is the epitome of their faith.

The second question is answered in a similar way. Its language also accords admirably with the new position of Christ. Its purport is also of a like definite and comprehensive description. 'Teach men to observe all things whatsoever I have commanded you.' The accepted disciple is always to rule himself by the precepts of Christ. That is the compendium of their duty.

The last answer teaches these teachers what to expect for themselves. Exceedingly arduous will that effort prove to which they are called. Possibly, exceedingly protracted as well. Whilst engaged in it, also, they must not expect to enjoy the visible presence of Christ. Yet, for all this, His effectual presence will be with them throughout. And the end of this effort, also, shall be the end of all their efforts and fears. 'Lo, I am with you always, even to the consummation of the age.' That is the summary of their hopes.

With this solemn 'charge' to His chosen successors and friends, this pioneer Life of Jesus of Nazareth is brought to its close.

Such a charge is at once a fitting close to His labours, and a fitting prelude to theirs.

Such a close, also, by connecting His history with the centuries since, carries us back to that opening genealogy of Jesus in this Gospel, which connected His history with the ages before.

In other words, the music terminates in the identical key in which it began.

PART VI.

THE SUMMING UP.

THE SUMMING UP.

IN this final section we desire to take a brief review of the main results of our Inquiry. What principal features have been traced by us in this earliest Story of Christ?

Its remarkable UNITY, as a literary production, would seem to come first. One central Figure, one consistent ideal, has been before us throughout. One great catastrophe, also, has been the master incident to which all else has led up.

The singular PERFECTION of the ideal presented to us appears to come next. Always consistent with itself, that ideal has also been always consistent with all that is lovely or great. Never feeble, yet never harsh; never haughty, yet never unworthy; never forced, yet never tame; there has never been in it, on either side, either excess or defect. There may be a fuller—there has never been a finer—conception of Christ.

Even in regard to this question of FULNESS, moreover, how striking a story this is! The bare headings of the successive divisions, to which our analysis of the work has led us, are enough to settle this point. Is there much of importance concerning Jesus of

Nazareth which these headings leave out? Is it not surprising, rather, in so contracted a space, to see how much they embrace?

Is it not equally surprising to see, in the next place, with what remarkable POWER this is done? How vivid and abiding are the impressions produced on us by the scenes and incidents of this story! How they arrest our attention; and compel our wonder; and dominate our emotions! Not even the most celebrated of those masterpieces of human art which are specially designed for these purposes succeed in doing so more. Is there anywhere, in reality, a sublimer *tragedy*—is there anywhere, in effect, a diviner *epic*—than this first story of Christ?

All the more wonderful, therefore, is the UTTER SIMPLICITY of its manner and style. We have not found a suspicion of 'art' in it, or a symptom of effort, from the first page to the last. With all the essentials, in fact, it has none of the pretensions of the highest productions of 'art.' Consequently, it has treble the worth.

Lastly, this story has been found to suggest to us even more than it shews. From its summit, as it were, we have made out the outlines of a succession of summits beyond. In its 'perturbations' we have detected the influence of remoter worlds still. In one sense the crucifixion of that innocent Jesus whom it portrays was like the consummation of all. In another sense, we felt it to be but the beginning of more.

Even the subsequent utter reversal of that strange calamity did not clear its mystery up. Rather, that final triumph only augmented the wonder of that antecedent disaster. Why did that Holy One who afterwards *raised Himself from the dead* submit to death on the cross?

Two questions present themselves, in view of these features, as the conclusion of all.

First, How are we to account for the existence among us of this highly exceptional Work?

According to the Christian view, the solution is to be found in the inspiration of the writer. He had a Divine Original from which to copy. He had Divine Help in so doing. Hence the perfection—the double perfection—of the result.

Is a simpler or better solution anywhere to be found?

Is there any other, indeed, which is really worthy of being placed by its side?

Next, In what direction are we to look for light in regard to the mystery of this story?

According to the Christian view, we are to look for it in another mystery yet. The reason why this Holy One of God, with all His power, was pleased to submit to all the horrors of the death of the cross, was because God had been pleased to lay upon Him—and He had been pleased to take on Himself—'the iniquity of us all.' In other words, because 'He bore our sins in His own body' on that mysterious 'tree.' In other words yet, because 'He died, the just for the unjust, that He might bring us to God.' It is in these 'remoter worlds' that *we* find the causes of the strange 'perturbation' of this.

Has any one ever yet suggested an equally adequate cause?

Is there any other explanation, indeed, which can even be said to grapple fairly with the real difficulties of the question?

Is there any other, also, which is equally worthy of the Christ of this book?

THE END.

www.ingramcontent.com/pod-product-compliance
Lightning Source LLC
Chambersburg PA
CBHW020246170426
43202CB00008B/254